A-Z

of
handy hints

A**CHOICE**BOOK

A**CHOICE**BOOK

Copyright © BOX PRESS 1998

First published in 1998 by CHOICE Books
57 Carrington Road Marrickville
NSW 2204 Australia

Reprinted 1998, 1999, 2000

National Library of Australia
Cataloguing-in-publication data
Bibby, Deborah
A-Z of handy hints: a choice book

Includes index
ISBN 0947277 41 2

1. Home Economics - Handbooks, manuals etc
I. James, Lisa . II. Title: A to Z of handy hints

640.41

Illustrations copyright © Alison Kubbos 1997
Printed in Australia by Griffin Press Pty Ltd

CONTENTS

ACKNOWLEDGMENTS

Many thanks to all family and
friends for their research, Rosh, Jill,
Cheryl, Joan, Breige, Bryn, Johann,
Phoebe (the green capiscum does go
red), Pete, and a special thanks to
Lynn for the many hints she
provided

INTRODUCTION

How do I get red wine out of my white shirt ?
What is the best way to keep mossies at bay
without chemical sprays ? I've run out of deodorant - didn't Grandma have an old tip ? How do
you keep weevils out of packaged food ? We've
heard it all before and struggle to remember that
crazy old tip Grandma told us about so long ago
and we wish we had a book filled with her handy
hints to keep on the kitchen shelf. That's where
this idea was born - out of sheer frustration.
There wasn't a book like it and we were positive
there would be hundreds like us who would love
to have one.

In these health and money conscious times,
natural everyday products come in handy -
you don't always have to turn to an expensive
chemical spray. Instead save on money and
look after your health. We decided to go back
to the good old days for inspiration and gathered
450 tried and tested handy hints from every
known source - grandmas, mothers, fathers,
boyfriends, aunts, uncles, friends, even the
odd stranger on the bus. We've had great fun
putting this book together and hope it saves
you hours of wracking your brain and solves
every dilemma in your home.

Deborah Bibby and Lisa James

artichoke

*perfect when heavy and
firm, and leaves are
tight*

A

ADHESIVE LABELS
To remove adhesive labels soak the label in water, or just cover with a wet cloth until the label is soaked through, then peel off.

Alternatively rub with nail-varnish remover (acetone).

AIR TRAVEL TIPS
Most tips for airline travel are common sense - but remember:

* Dress for comfort when travelling. Wear loose fitting clothes and easy fitting shoes, as feet swell during travel. If you want to smarten up on arrival, carry clothing to change into. There are always plenty of toilets, lounges and bathrooms at airports for this.

* Less is definitely best when it comes to eating. You do not have to eat all the meals served to you. Skip one and feel the benefit at the end of the journey.

* The same applies to wine and spirits. Limit your intake and drink water whenever possible. This will prevent you from feeling dehydrated in the air pressurised cabin.

* Your skin will dry out in the cabin air. Before you leave for the airport, apply moisturiser to your face and body. Water atomisers are effective - but only if applied freely and often during flight.

ALMONDS
The skin is hard to get off most of the time, but if you pour boiling water over them and leave them to stand for four minutes, then drain and rub them between your fingers - the skin falls off easily.

To cut almonds into strips do so when they are damp from having been skinned.

To give almonds a golden look dust with powdered sugar before grilling.

ALUMINIUM

Aluminium window frames can get black pitted marks on them - it looks like mould. The best way to clean is with hot soapy water and soap-impregnated steel wool pads. Rub hard in one direction to avoid scratching. You could also try some crumpled-up tin foil.

ANIMAL HAIR

To remove animal hair from clothes or furniture, wrap sticky tape around your fingers (sticky side up) and rub over surface - it works wonderfully.

ANIMAL STAINS (urine, excreta, vomit)

Scrape the surface deposit and then sponge with cold water. Soak in a solution of borax and warm water (one tablespoon borax to 1/2 litre of water). Leave to soak for about one hour.

On the carpet: Scrape the surface as before and then blot it dry with absorbent paper. Next rub with a mixture of vinegar and warm soapy water (1/2 litre water and two tablespoons vinegar). Blot dry and then splash with soda water. Blot dry again and rub over with a cloth, dampened with ammonia.

Now you can leave it alone and let it dry. Another trick is to blot dry and pour methylated spirits on it, rub and then blot dry. Raise the pile and allow to dry.

ANKLES

To relieve ankles that are swelling you can't beat ice. Pack tightly into a plastic bag, wrap in a light towel and place against the swollen area. If swelling has not subsided after a few hours (or it reoccurs) consult your doctor.

ANTS

To deter ants sprinkle bicarbonate of soda on shelves and in drawers.

To get rid of them, find out where they are coming in and sprinkle mint, chilli powder, pepper or borax across their trail.

By planting mint close to doors, windows and other entrances you will keep them away as ants don't like the smell !

ANT NESTS

If you are keen to stop ants, find their nest and scatter the area with a powder made up of one part borax and one part icing sugar. Borax will poison the ants but is harmless to humans and animals.

APHIDS

Keep aphids off your rose bushes by planting chives, garlic and parsley close to them.

These plants provide a natural and effective way of repelling aphids without the use of chemical sprays.

APPLES

Apples will keep if they are rubbed with glycerine before storing (make sure the storing area is cool and ventilated, store with the stalk end up). To keep apples from browning once cut, put in a bowl of cold water until ready to use.

AQUARIUMS

If you are new to goldfish you'll appreciate the following hints:

* Only ever half-fill a round goldfish bowl with water so the surface area of the water will be greater than if filled to the top. This will leave your fish with more oxygen and so healthier.

* If the fish become a permanent feature you should keep them in a rectangular container.

* When filling the aquarium with water, in order not to disturb the gravel, try placing a cup on the bottom and pour the water into the cup. It will gently overflow and fill up without disturbing anything.

ARTICHOKE

How to select a good artichoke - the trick is in the leaves. If they are tight and the artichoke is heavy and firm - it is perfect. However, if the leaves are open it will be tasteless.

When cooking artichokes if you add a dash of lemon juice or vinegar to the cooking water you will bring out the beautiful flavour.

ARTIFICIAL FLOWERS

To freshen them up, steam over a shallow pan of boiling water or hold over the steam of a kettle and then carefully reshape.

NB - This does not apply to paper flowers.

ASPARAGUS

When opening a tin of asparagus, open the tin from the bottom and the asparagus will slide out bottom first instead of head first which damages the tips.

AVOCADO

Isn't it frustrating when you buy that expensive avocado and it's either overripe or hard as a rock. These hints should help:

* Don't buy an avocado with black spots because it is too ripe.

* If you are buying one to be eaten that same day, press the stalk end gently and if it is soft you've got a ripe one.

* If you have bought a hard avocado wrap it in a brown paper bag and place it in a warm spot in the kitchen.

* To store half an avocado brush the cut end with lemon juice; this will stop it going brown. Leave the stone in and cover with cling wrap.

B

bottle

place rubber bands
around slippery bottles
to handle safely

B

BABY SICK SMELL
Dab the affected clothes with sodium bicarbonate and when dry brush off.

BABY SLEEPING
If baby's sleep is disturbed at night for feeding or any other reason, fill a hot water bottle with warm (not too hot) water, and place in the cot. Remove the hot water bottle before putting baby back in the cot. This will keep the bedding warm and help baby either stay asleep, or go back to sleep when returned to the cot.

BACKACHE
Some back problems are caused by lifting heavy objects incorrectly. Avoid problems with your back by lifting properly. Stand firm with your feet slightly apart. Bend your knees and hips, using your strong leg muscles to lift. Get a good grip on the load, and keep it close to your body. Keep your back as straight as possible during the whole lift.

NEVER bend your spine forward when lifting.

BACON
To unstick frozen bacon rashers and separate them, heat a metal spatula in boiling water and then slide between the bacon slices.

If bacon is too salty make it edible by soaking in milk for five minutes before grilling.

Wrap it in foil instead of plastic wrap. Bacon will stay fresher for longer this way.

BAD BREATH

Avoid bad breath by brushing your teeth as often as possible during the day and after meals, or try the following:

* To quickly remedy bad breath crunch on a clove. Your breath will smell as sweet as a carnation.

  Cloves can be easily carried around with you for this purpose.

* Put 1/2 teaspoon of essence of cinnamon into half a glass of warm water and use as a mouth wash.

The well-known trick is of course chewing fresh parsley and it works.

To avoid bad breath, eat three meals a day as skipping meals allows bacteria to build up in the mouth, causing bad breath.

This might sound strange but brushing your tongue, as well as your teeth also helps your breath stay fresh.

BAKING POWDER

Sometimes this sits in the cupboard for months opened, but unused. To check if baking powder is still fresh add a teaspoonful to a quarter litre of water. If it gets very effervescent, it is still fresh. If not, you need a new batch.

BAKING TINS

To delay any rusting rub inside and out with lard then place in a warm oven for 40 minutes. Let cool and then wipe with paper towel. To remove rust, rub baking tins with a cut raw potato dipped in a scouring powder. Rinse and dry.

BALLOON TYING

The plastic clips from bread bags are ideal, and a real time saver for tying balloons.

Blow up balloon, and push the neck through the plastic clip. Wrap around once and clip into place.

BALLPOINT INK STAIN

For washable fabrics, soak in methylated spirits and then wash as normal.

BANANAS

You cannot keep bananas in the freezer, they go black. But you can mash overripe bananas and freeze them by adding a little lemon juice when mashing. Handy when next making a banana cake.

BANANA SAP STAINS

Cover the stained area with dry borax and then run hot water through the material.

BARBECUE PLATE

So greasy it's hard to clean?

Just sprinkle salt on it while still hot, allow to cool and then clean - much easier. To clean, wash with a soft brush dipped in salt water. Dry with a soft cloth and then rub over with linseed oil.

BASIL

Don't you find when cooking a dish that requires basil leaves you have to buy a bunch of basil and never need it all for the dish ? And it seems to go limp and lifeless so quickly that you end up throwing it out - what a waste!

Well next time try this:

Put the remainder of your cleaned basil leaves into a rectangular container, sprinkle with salt and shake. Now fill with olive or vegetable oil. Cover and store in the fridge. They will last for months and months. Use as required.

BATH
To clean, use warm soapy water and a few tablespoons of vinegar.

BATHROOM MIRRORS
Wipe over with glycerine - they will remain fog free after those steamy showers and baths.

BATH STAINS
After cleaning and drying the bath, rub it over with sodium bicarbonate on a damp cloth then polish by wiping with white vinegar.

BATTER MIXING TIP
For those of you who make your own batter, wind an elastic band around the handle of your wooden spoon. It will grip the side of the bowl and save you fishing the spoon out of the mixture or leaving drops all over your kitchen.

BATTERIES
If they're loose in your Walkman, radio, etc., because of a missing or defective spring get a piece of foil and push it into the defective end. This will secure the battery and restore contact.

BATTERY TERMINALS
Mix several teaspoons of sodium bicarbonate with a litre of water and apply to terminals to remove all acid build up.

BEADS (threading)

Does the thought of re-stringing a beaded necklace make you keep putting it off? Try this - stick the new thread to the old thread with nail varnish or super glue; once dry pull the old thread out carefully.

Children love playing with and threading beads, but when the thread is limp they may quickly lose their patience. Try dipping the end of the thread in nail varnish and leave to dry. Now the thread will be stiff enough to easily pass through the beads.

* Dental floss is also great for kids to string beads and so too are long shoe laces and fishing line.

* Some shells make great beads for kids as do macaroni shapes dipped in different food colourings.

BEANSPROUTS

Beansprouts stay fresher for longer if stored in the fridge, in a bowl of water with a few slices of lemon in it.

BEES

A bee in the house - get a flower and he'll buzz straight to it. When he settles on it take the flower outdoors or shake out the window. If you cannot get a flower fill a saucer with sugared or honeyed water and he'll make a beeline for it.

BEETROOT STAINS

Rinse with cold water then stretch fabric over any container. Sprinkle with powdered borax and then pour boiling water through it.

Or fill a shallow bowl with milk and place the stained cloth in the milk - now this might seem ridiculous but it's worth trying.

Put a slice of bread on top of the milk-soaked portion of cloth and it absorbs the stain. Leave for five minutes and then wash as usual.

BETTER BROOMS
Sprinkle a little kerosone on your broom once a week and it will collect fluff and dust much more easily.

BIRD DROPPINGS
Soak in a nappy treatment and then wash. If the stain remains dab with hydrogen peroxide.

On canvas garden furniture - Brush any deposit and rub stain with household soap. Leave for 1/2 hour and rinse well. You may need to repeat this.

On carpet - Brush up any deposit, then sponge with ammonia and water (one teacup water to one tablespoon ammonia). Then sponge again with white vinegar and rinse. All should be well again.

On balcony or deck - If the rain doesn't wash it away, wait until it is dry and then using a chisel or screwdriver chip it off.

BISCUITS
Do not keep biscuits in the same tin as cake as they will go soggy.

BLACKBOARD (cleaning)
Keep a blackboard clean by sponging occasionally with ammonia. This should remove any build up of dust or dirt and keep the surface good for writing on. It will also remove wax crayon.

BLACK CLOTHES (fading)
Prevent your black clothes from fading by adding a few drops of vinegar to the water when washing.

BLACK EYE
Mix a teacup of hot water with a heaped tablespoon of bicarbonate of soda. Cover the eye lightly with cotton wool dipped in the solution.

BLISTERS
If you do a lot of walking or running and suffer blisters try this one. Rub your feet in methylated spirits daily for a week beforehand and it should do the trick.

BLOCKED SINK OR DRAIN
Mix a tablespoon of bicarbonate of soda with three tablespoons of vinegar and pour into the blocked sink or drain. Leave for a minute and then pour in a kettle full of boiling water. This will help clear the blockage and also make the sink smell new again.

BLOOD STAIN
Soak in cold water, then wash as normal. If the stain persists soak in bleach and warm water, or warm water and a nappy treatment. If a brown mark still remains dab with hydrogen peroxide until it disappears.

BLUEBOTTLE STING
Although not a matter of life and death, a bluebottle sting causes a great deal of pain. Their long tentacles wrap around you and it is best not to struggle as the tentacles break off and can end up in your eyes or mouth. Treat a sting by washing with hot, water, as hot as you can stand. Then apply an antiseptic cream. DO NOT RUB WITH SAND - this only makes it worse. **Seek medical attention as soon as possible.**

BOAT KEYS
Just in case you hadn't thought of it - make sure your boat keys are always attached to a floating key holder.

BOOKS
Some sprigs of thyme behind the books on your shelf will keep silverfish and other insects away.

Don't dust the top of your books with a damp cloth, instead use a wide clean paint brush.

To remove grease spots from the page of a book, place a piece of blotting paper on either side of the page and press with a warm iron. The blotting paper will absorb the grease.

A torn page can be repaired with the white of an egg! Smear the tear lightly with egg white and leave to dry.

To keep a leather bound book in good condition polish once a year with any of the following: saddle soap, leather wax, petroleum jelly or colourless wax.

Your treasured book has a hole in one of its pages? Try this - chew a piece of paper until soft, press into the hole and then iron this with a warm iron.

BOOTS (knee-high)
You'll need this tip to look after knee-high boots: Grab an old magazine (quite thick) roll it up an insert into the boot. The magazine will unfold to the width of the boot and this will keep its great shape. By the way never dry wet leather boots or shoes near an open fire as the leather will harden.

BOTTLES

Bottles containing oil can be slippery. Place some rubber bands around them to avoid accidents.

To clean a very dirty bottle, pour a little flour into the bottle to line the bottom. Next fill up slowly (be careful) with hot water. Leave overnight and rinse the next day.

To get rid of a strong smell in a bottle fill with cold water and four teaspoons of dry mustard. Leave overnight and then rinse well. The bottle will now be fresh to smell.

To prevent a bottle from cracking when pouring anything hot into it stand the bottle on a warm damp cloth or put a knife under the bottle.

BOX JELLYFISH STING

These are found in the shallow waters of northern Australia and can cause a serious sting. The toxin they produce may cause respiratory and heart problems.

If stung, try to get out of the water slowly - as the jellyfish will actually move out of your way.

Wash the area with salt water and then soak in hot water, as hot as you can stand.

Seek medical attention immediately.

BREAD

Stale bread can be brought back to life by dipping very quickly in water, then pop into a hot oven wrapped in foil for a minute.

BRICKS
To clean dirty bricks around the fireplace scrub with a brush and malt vinegar, then rinse.

BROOMS
If your broom has gone too soft you can harden the bristles by soaking in an equal solution of white vinegar and water.

A few drops of kerosene on a soft broom once a week will collect fluff and dust more easily.

BROWN SUGAR
To keep it from going hard and dry put it in a tin and place three marshmallows on top and keep lid tightly closed.

To soften hard brown sugar place it in a warm oven or microwave until soft again.

BROWNING BANANAS
After peeling bananas, hold them under a cold running tap and they will not go brown. Or squeeze lemon juice over them.

BURNT MILK
Add a pinch of salt to burnt milk and it will take away the scorched taste.

BURNT SAUCEPANS
Make a bicarbonate of soda and water paste, cover burnt area of saucepan and leave overnight. Next morning rub clean.

BURNT TOAST
If you burn the toast and still want to use it, rub the two slices together. This will get rid of the burnt black and leave the toast in better condition than if you scrape it.

BUTTER

To keep butter fresh and firm when at a picnic or on the afternoon lunch table wrap it in fresh cabbage leaves.

Hard butter taken from the fridge may also be softened quickly by cutting it up roughly and pouring water from the cold tap over it. Allow to stand for a few minutes then pour off the water - the butter will be ready for spreading.

BUTTERMILK

When a recipe requires buttermilk and you have none, add a splash of vinegar to milk and it will do the trick perfectly.

BUTTONS

Shine up metal buttons on jackets and blazers by rubbing with a cottonwool ball dampened with vinegar.

C

cough

a mixture of garlic &
honey will provide
natural relief

C

CAKE

When cutting a sponge cake for filling - use a length of cotton thread - it's finer than a knife and actually slices the cake much neater.

CAKE (dry)

If you overcook a fruit or butter cake, and it is dry when it comes out of the oven, leave to cool with a thick folded towel over the top of the cake. This will soften the cake considerably.

CAKE (storing)

Store your cakes in upside down tins. Put cake on top of lid and use the base as a cover. This makes it easier to cut and remove the cake.

CAKE TINS

Put a whole or cut lemon in the cake tin and it will prevent the cake from drying out.

CANDLE WAX

Never scrape candle wax off a wooden table or surface with a sharp knife, use a strong cardboard. Then wipe the remaining wax with a cloth dampened with paraffin.

CANDLES

Stop dripping candles by putting them in the fridge for 48 hours before lighting. When thoroughly chilled they burn down only an inch in an hour.

CANE
Keep cane furniture looking good by wiping with a solution of equal parts of vinegar and water. Dry cane outside, in warm weather, if possible.

CAPSICUM
Red capsicums are more expensive than green ones so make your own by putting a green capsicum in a brown bag with a banana and it will go red.

CAR SICKNESS
You can sometimes avoid car sickness by freshening the air inside the car with a cut lemon placed on top of the dashboard. Or try a few sprigs of fresh or dried lavender spread around.

CAR TRAVELLING
Never read when travelling in cars and buses. It makes you feel sick.

CARPETS (spring clean recipe)
Sprinkle with equal parts cornflour and bicarbonate of soda. Leave for about an hour and then vacuum.

CATS ON CARS
Keep neighbourhood cats off your car by sprinkling it with pepper when unused for a while.

CATS IN GARDEN
Keep cats out for your garden by putting chopped fresh lemons amongst the plants. Cats hate the smell and won't come near it.

CHAMOIS LEATHER
To keep it soft and supple store in a glass jar with or without the lid.

CHAPPED HANDS
If hands are chapped, rinse them with a little vinegar each time you wash them. Don't rinse vinegar off - just pat dry. The smell will soon fade.

OR Rub your hands with the yellow side of lemon peel, then rinse and dry thoroughly.

CHEWING GUM STUCK IN HAIR
Dab with a cloth soaked in eucalyptus oil.

CHEWING GUM STUCK ON CLOTH
Apply egg white to gum to soften and then pick off as much as possible. Wash as normal - good luck!

You can also remove chewing gum by applying eucalyptus oil to the fabric, then wash as normal.

CHILDREN'S POTTY
Wash out with vinegar or bicarbonate of soda to keep fresh.

CHIPS
Of the French Fried variety - if they're not browning in the oil add a drop of vinegar to speed up the process.

CHOCOLATE CRACKLES
Instead of using paper cupcake holders, spoon the chocolate crackle mixture into flat based ice cream cones. The children love them !

CHOCOLATE STAIN
Soak in borax and warm water and then wash (30g borax to 1 litre water).

CHRISTMAS TREE
Keep your real Christmas tree healthy throughout the Christmas period by standing tree in a bucket filled half and half with sand and soil. Water regularly and keep the mixture damp at all times.

This will ensure the tree does not lose so many needles and it will stay looking fresh and green for longer.

OR Try spraying pine needles heavily with a home-made hairspray (see page 65 for recipe) to prevent them from falling off. Do this outside before standing tree in the bucket of soil and placing inside.

CHRISTMAS TREE DECORATIONS
When packing some fragile decorations away use egg cartons for extra safety.

CHRISTMAS TREE RESIN
The resin from your Christmas tree is easily removed from your hands by rubbing them with dry bicarbonate of soda and then rinsing.

CHUTNEY (home-made)
If you run out of chutney try mixing together Worcestershire sauce and plum jam. Add sultanas to taste for a quick and easy alternative.

CLEAN CAR WINDOWS
Use a cut raw potato to clean your car windows first thing in the morning. This works especially well on foggy days and helps to keep the windows clear.

CLEANER (environmentally friendly - all purpose)
Make your own ' green-clean' spray for use around the home.

Mix together 50ml of vinegar, 50ml of cloudy ammonia, and 120ml of bicarbonate of soda with 4 litres of hot water. Keep solution in a pump action spray bottle and shake well before use.

Solution can also be applied directly with a cloth.

CLOTHES LINE
If you're short of space peg socks to a wire coat hanger and hang on the line or peg it on.

COCKROACH PROBLEM
* Half fill an empty unwashed butter or margarine container with beer or wine, and leave it out for the cockroaches. Yes, they love alcohol and dive into the container but they can't get out as it's too slippery and they drown.

* You can also grease the inner neck of a milk bottle and place a little stale beer in it - they climb in but will not be able to get out.

* A light dusting of borax around the fridge, stove and places frequented by cockroaches will also control a cockroach problem.

* Send cockroaches packing with the green skins of cucumbers. Spread skin around the floor, at night, in areas cockroaches frequent and after 3 to 4 nights in a row, they won't come back.

COCKROACH REPELLENT
Make your own environmentally friendly cockroach pastes to keep them away.

Mix flour with cocoa and borax and leave in shallow dishes at night. Bicarbonate of soda mixed with sugar can also be used.

KEEP BOTH WELL AWAY FROM CHILDREN AND PETS.

COFFEE PERCOLATOR (cleaning)
Clean your electric coffee percolator by filling with cold water mixed with 5 tablespoons of bicarbonate of soda. Turn on and allow to boil and complete normal cycle. Then turn off and leave to stand for 10 minutes. Wash as usual, rinse and dry.

COLDS
If you have a cold and are suffering from a blocked nose and cannot sleep at night, warm your ears with a hot compress (as hot as you can handle). Keep it on for at least ten minutes, your nose will unblock and you'll fall fast asleep.

COMBS
Dirty combs can be cleaned by placing them in a small amount of hot water and sprinkling with a teaspoon of bicarbonate of soda. Leave for three minutes and viola!

COMPUTER CARE
To keep your computer screen and keyboard clean and free of dust, use a soft damp cloth and rub with methylated spirits.

CONSTIPATION
Two heaped teaspoonfuls of unprocessed bran from your health food shop mixed in with your breakfast cereal in the morning will correct the problem.

CONTACT LENSES

Find a dropped contact lens by covering the end of a vacuum cleaner with a stocking and securing with an elastic band. Then vacuum the floor in the area where the lens was dropped. The lens will be sucked up onto the stocking and stick to it.

This works well for other small objects such as earrings, a lost gemstone etc.

COUGH

Treat a catarrh-like cough with a syrup made from honey and garlic - and it tastes much better than you think. Finely slice 4 cloves of garlic and mix with 4 tablespoons of honey in a jar. Stir well and leave in the jar for 2 hours. The mixture will infuse and you should then take 2 teaspoons of the juice, four times a day. This is a natural and very effective treatment.

CREAKING DOOR

To stop those annoying door creaks, apply soap to the hinges.

CREAKING FLOORBOARDS

Sprinkle talcum powder between the floorboards to prevent squeaking. Repeat as necessary.

CREAM

A pinch of bicarbonate of soda mixed into cream will prevent it from going sour. A wonderful tip if you are using the cream to fill a cake.

Cream that is too thin for whipping can be whipped if you add a few drops of lemon juice and allow to stand for a few minutes before beating.

CREAM (mock)
Particularly useful for dieters - this recipe is for making cream that tastes like cream, looks like cream, but has much less fat.

Blend together 1 tablespoon of cornflour, and 2 tablespoons of cold milk until smooth. Heat a cup of milk in a saucepan and add the milk and cornflour mix.

Stir whilst bringing to the boil, then simmer for 2 minutes, stirring all the time. Leave to cool. Then cream together 1 tablespoon of butter, 1 tablespoon of castor sugar and a few drops of vanilla essence. Add the cool milk and beat together.

CRICKET WHITES
For sparkling white pants wash in a solution of equal parts cloudy ammonia and water. With really difficult stains (like the red stains from the cricket ball) add a teaspoon of methylated spirits. A nappy treatment will keep pants bright and white too.

CRISPY CHICKEN SKIN
Rub a small amount of mayonnaise into the chicken skin before cooking to make the skin crisp and golden.

CURRY STAINS
Soak stained area in diluted ammonia.

D

damaged hair

revitalise it with a
lotion of raw eggs &
lemon juice

D

DAMAGED HAIR

Try this natural and home made lotion for your dry and damaged hair. Mix 2 tablespoons of vinegar or lemon juice with 2 raw eggs, until fluffy. Wash your hair and rinse it well.

Towel dry and then work the mixture through your hair using your hands. Leave for 15 minutes and then wash with lukewarm (not hot) water.

DAMPNESS (cupboards)

Keep your linen cupboard dry and free of any musty odours, with a small jar full of cloves placed inside the cupboard. A jar full of salt will also do the trick.

DAMPNESS (rooms)

If the room feels damp place a piece of camphor in the corners. Leave for at least a week, or until the camphor has evaporated and the room will no longer feel damp.

DANDRUFF

Massage olive oil and sulphur (equal parts) into the scalp, leave for an hour and then shampoo. Sometimes dandruff can be caused due to a lack of vitamin B. Check out your dietary intake.

DECORATING CAKES

To decorate a cake in a hurry, place an open-work paper doily on top of the cake and sprinkle well with icing sugar. Remove doily carefully.

DEODORANT
If you've run out of deodorant apply bicarbonate of soda under arms after bath or shower - it's a great deodorant.

DISHWASHER (deodoriser)
To refresh your dishwasher and to get rid of any unwelcome odours pour 4 heaped tablespoons of bicarbonate of soda into the washer and run through the rinse cycle.

DISHWASHER DETERGENTS
Instead of commercial detergents, try a natural alternative. Washing soda can be used for detergent, and vinegar as a rinse aid will reduce spotting and streaks.

DOG AND CAT HAIRS
These hairs are hard to get off the carpet, but this method works wonders. Use a damp mop and lightly mop the carpet surface. Then vacuum and watch the hairs come up easily.

DOOR (that sticks)
Doors contract and expand with changes in the weather and so the problem may come and go. If this is the case, simply rub a candle along the edge that jams.

If the door sticks all the time, the problem edge will need sanding. Make this easier by wrapping a piece of sandpaper around a block of wood and rubbing.

If the door sticks at the bottom, tape a coarse piece of sandpaper to the floor and push the door back and forth until it glides easily over it.

DRAWERS (that stick)

To stop an ill fitting drawer from sticking, rub the bottom sides with sandpaper. Finish off with a coat of floor polish both on the drawer and along the sides, and polish well.

OR If drawers are sticking rub a little floor polish along the sides and polish.

DRIED FRUIT

To stop dried fruit and glace cherries from sinking to the bottom of your fruit cake mix, toss them in cornflour before adding to the mixture.

DRY CLEANING

Try to avoid dry cleaning, as the process used to clean in this way uses toxic chemicals which are bad for you, your clothes and the environment.

Most fabrics may be washed in the normal way. Manufacturers often label items 'dry clean only' for their own protection.

DRY HAIR

Very dry and difficult hair will improve in texture and look if conditioned with olive oil or coconut oil. First warm the oil and spread it generously over your hair. Wrap head in a warm towel and leave for an hour. Then shampoo as usual.

DRYING FLOWERS

Flowers with fragile petals should be dried on silver sand (available from builders' suppliers). Place the flower on sand in a box, cover with more sand and leave for a week.

You can also use borax powder and sand and talcum powder also works.

With talcum powder cover the base of a tin with talc, place the flowers in and fill with talc. Make sure all air is excluded. Leave for fifteen days.

DUSTERS
Soak in turpentine and then leave to dry. You'll be amazed how much more dust they collect.

E

eggs

*easier to whisk with
a pinch of salt*

E

EGG CARTONS
Your empty egg cartons make perfect storage containers. Try
using them for storing reels of cotton, or those fiddly bits and
pieces in your drawers.

EGGS
To test whether or not your eggs are still fresh, place in a pan of
cold water. A fresh egg will sink to the bottom and stay there.
A stale egg will float on the top.

Store eggs with their larger end facing down. They will stay
fresher longer.

EGGS (boiled)
When using eggs for salad, boil as usual and then plunge in cold
water before peeling. This will prevent egg yolks from turning
greyish.

Test for a hard boiled egg by blowing on the egg shell as soon as
you take it out of the water. If the shell dries immediately, it is
ready. If the shell remains wet, the yolk is still soft and it needs
more cooking.

To peel boiled eggs, tap top and then roll egg back and forth a
few times before peeling off shell. This makes it easier to do.

EGGS (poaching)
When poaching eggs add a tablespoon of vinegar to the pan to
prevent the yolks breaking.

EGGS (whisking)
Add a small pinch of salt (no more) to egg whites before beating - they will whisk quicker and better.

Always use egg whites stored at room temperature for whisking. Cold eggs from the fridge do not give the same volume.

EGG WHITES
Use a small funnel to separate egg whites from the yolk. Crack egg directly into funnel and watch the white run through whilst the yolk stays there.

ELBOWS
Scrub rough and hardened elbows with a nail brush dipped in hot water and a mild soap. Dry and then massage with olive oil.

Alternatively, squeeze out two halves of a lemon. Add a little olive oil and lean elbows in them for 10-15 minutes. Rinse with warm water and massage in a moisturiser.

ELECTRIC JUG
Clean your electric jug by half filling with cold water, and add a quarter cup of white vinegar to it. Bring to the boil, and leave for 30 seconds. Repeat procedure twice and then rinse.

ENAMEL WARE
Stains may be removed from enamel ware with a soft cloth, dipped first in salt and then moistened with turpentine.

Another method - for light stains only - is to dampen a soft cloth and dip in baking soda.

For really heavy stains try rubbing with a strong chlorine-based bleach. Wash down on completion.

EUCALYPTUS OIL

Is useful in many ways around the home. Try cleaning a dark coloured bath immediately after use with a cloth that has been wrung out in hot water and then sprinkled with eucalyptus oil. It will get rid of any marks and keep the bath shining.

Eucalyptus oil is also great for cleaning chrome taps and towel rails using the same method.

EYES (puffy)

Try placing a slice of cold cucumber on each eye and leave for two minutes.

OR Brew a cup of herbal tea with two herbal teabags. Leave them to cool while you enjoy the brew and then relax further by placing one on each eye for 5 -10 minutes. If you're out of teabags and cucumber place slices of cold raw potato over each eye.

OR Place a teaspoon in the freezer and when cold wrap it in a tissue and press the convex side of the spoon underneath your eye for a minute.

EYES (sore or tired)

Bathe eyes with cotton wool soaked in fennel or herbal tea.

F

flowers

cut poppies as soon
as petals begin to
show.

F

FACE STEAM
To clear and freshen your skin, put a handful of fresh peppermint leaves in a bowl and cover with boiling water (peppermint acts as an antiseptic and stimulates the circulation). Cover your head and the bowl with a large towel and steam away. Stay there as long as the steam lasts. Pat dry.

FAT FREE FRUIT CAKE
For those weightwatchers who enjoy a slice of something sweet now and then, here's a recipe for a cake without sugar or butter, that still tastes great.

You will need:
- 250g chopped dates
- 4 tablespoons of orange juice
- 1 egg
- 500g mixed fruit
- 125g plain flour
- 60g self-raising flour
- 60g ground almonds
- 2 teaspoons baking powder
- 1 teaspoon spice
- 1/4 cup almonds

Method: Place chopped dates in a saucepan, cover with water and simmer for 5 minutes until soft. Allow to cool then add 4 tablespoons of orange juice and stir. Then add a beaten egg and the mixed fruit and put to one side.

Place the flour, ground almonds, baking powder, spice and almonds in a bowl and mix together. Add the dry ingredients to the cooled mixture and mix well.

Place into a large, lined loaf tin and bake for 1 1/4 hours at
170 C. This is an old English recipe.

FEET (tired)
After washing and drying your tired or aching feet, dab them
with methylated spirits on some cotton wool for an instant lift.

Another tip for tired feet: soak in warm water with three
tablespoons of vinegar - this brings great relief

FELT-TIP PENS
If your felt-tip pen has become dry - dip the tip in vinegar and
this will keep it working a little longer.

To retain felt-tip pens in good working order store them with the
caps on - tip down in a glass jar.

FINGER-PAINT
To make your own environmentally safe finger-paint try this:

1 tablespoon cornflour mixed with a little water to form a milky,
thick paste. Next add some boiling water stirring quickly.

Repeat this and once again stir very quickly until you have a
smooth, thick paste. Now just add food colouring and allow to
cool before giving to children to paint with.

(If mixture does not thicken to a consistency that you like try
cooking for a minute on the stove.)

FIRE-MAKING
Do not use coloured papers or magazines for lighting a fire as
the coloured ink may give off some lead vapour when burning.

To avoid smoke and wood burning odours, throw orange and lemon peels into the fire.

FISH BATTER
For a non-greasy fish batter add one part vinegar with three parts water and 3/4 teaspoon of baking soda to your usual batter recipe. It will brown quickly and not be greasy.

FISHTANK (cleaning)
To give your fish tank a good clean, scrub the empty tank with salt. Rinse thoroughly before refilling. It will leave the tank sparkling clean.

FISHY SMELLS IN A SAUCEPAN
You can get rid of these by emptying tea leaves into the pan and covering with water. Leave for several minutes and then rinse.

FLANNELETTE
To prevent fluff on new flannelette sheets, wash them in a solution of salt and vinegar. Mix a tablespoon of salt with a teacup of vinegar and add to your normal wash.

FLEAS
Controlling fleas on pets is the key to stopping your home from becoming infested. Give animals herbal baths and use a flea comb regularly. By rubbing your pet with a mixture of olive oil and a few drops of lavender, thyme or eucalyptus oil you will put fleas off. Replace any bedding for your pet with old cotton sheets or newspaper to reduce infestation.

If fleas have become a problem in your home, there is nothing for it but to clean out the entire house. Vacuum clean regularly, and empty the vacuum each time. Remember that flea eggs can hatch between 2-12 days in warm conditions.

Once you've got rid of them, keep rooms 'flea-free' by vacuuming regularly and sprinkling infested areas with lavender oil.

FLIES
Keep flies away by sprinkling ammonia on newspaper and rub on windows. They'll also stay away if you grow basil in pots and place in the kitchen.

OR keep flies away from the house by cleaning windows with a cloth soaked in kerosene. Leave to dry for 10 minutes and then polish with a clean, dry cloth.

To get rid of flies in the house, place balls of cotton wool sprinkled with a few drops of lavender oil in saucers around the house.

To keep flies at bay in the kitchen or outdoor eating areas, plant spearmint, peppermint and basil in pots. This will repel them.

FLOOR PROTECTORS
Bunion pads make great protectors and prevent floor scratching if stuck to the bottom of furniture (i.e. chair legs, tables legs). Try sticking them to the bottom of small ornaments and objects on cupboards, dressers, shelves etc. to spare these surfaces too.

Another great way to protect your wooden floors before moving furniture is to slip heavy socks over the legs of tables or chairs. This is also great for a laugh.

FLOORS (dirty)
To clean dirty varnished floors, wash with a mop dipped into a solution of warm water and half a cup of methylated spirits.

For wooden floors, avoid cleaning with very hot water, strong soaps and sodas as this will turn them yellow.

Marks left by furniture legs should be rubbed with a damp cloth dipped in paraffin or kerosene. If very dirty, scrub with steel wool dipped in turpentine.

Vinyl or linoleum floors will shine if paraffin is added to the water when washing. Black marks on lino can be removed by rubbing with a pencil eraser.

FLOORS (scratched)
Scratches on varnished floors should be rubbed over with a little lard and polished with a clean cloth.

To remove marks from a vinyl floor rub with bicarbonate of soda on a damp cloth.

FLOUR
If your flour happens to be in a unmarked container and you have forgotten if it's self-raising or plain, try this trick; place a teaspoon of the flour into a cup of water. If it bubbles to the surface it is self-raising, if it doesn't - you guessed it, it's definitely plain flour.

FLOUR (self-raising)
Turn your plain flour into self-raising flour by adding 4 level tablespoons of baking powder to one kilogram of flour (or 1 level tablespoon to 250g of flour and 2 for 500g, 3 for 750g). Mix well and use as for self-raising flour recipes.

FLOWERS (how to get rid of that old water smell)
Do you always hold your nose when tossing old cut flowers out of their vase? Just put a splash of bleach into the water before adding fresh flowers and the water will always smell fresh.

FLOWERS (and when to cut)
Gladioli should be cut when the second flower begins to open.

Irises should be cut when the first bud begins to unfold.

Cut poppies as soon as petals begin to show.

FLY SCREENS
Usually a nightmare to clean. Try dusting with the brush attachment of your vacuum cleaner or a simple hand brush. Next, rub both sides of the screen with a cloth dipped in paraffin oil (the paraffin prevents the wire rusting).

If you get a hole in the screen you can repair by painting it with nail polish. Leave the varnish to dry and paint again and again.

FOOD ADDITIVES
It is handy to know what is meant by food additives.

They are used in the preparation of food either to add to its flavour, colour, feel, and look, and also to keep products fresher for longer. There are 5 categories.

These are:

*   PRESERVATIVES which restrict the growth of bacteria that would cause the food to rot or become toxic if not added.

*   ANTIOXIDANTS - added to stop oils and fats from turning sour. This prolongs the shelf life of foods containing these items.

*   COSMETIC - added to alter the taste, look and texture of food.

*   PROCESSING - used in processing and packaging to help with the procedure i.e anti-foaming or clarifying agents.

*   NUTRIENTS - these are vitamins, minerals and calcium added to foods to enhance their content.

Salt & sugar are the most commonly added ingredients and your intake of both should be controlled.

FOUNTAIN PEN
Before writing with a fountain pen that has not been used for a while, flush the pen with ammonia followed by warm water. This will remove any clotted and dried ink. Shake well to remove excess water, before filling with fresh ink.

FREEZER (defrosting)
When defrosting the freezer, wipe it over with glycerine before turning back on.

Next time you defrost it, the ice will peel off quickly and easily.

FREEZING FOOD
Put sheets of waxed paper between pieces of meat and fish fillets before freezing and they'll be easy to separate.

FRIDGE (cleaning)
Rub inside with a solution made up of 1/2 a cup of vinegar and 1/4 a cup of bicarbonate of soda. This will prevent mildew and keep the fridge smelling fresh and free of food odours.

OR Clean as above and finish off by rubbing over with a few drops of vanilla essence on a slightly damp cloth.

FRIDGE ODOURS
Put a teaspoon of bicarbonate of soda in a small glass of water
and place in the fridge. It will smell fresh for several weeks.
You should also clean your fridge with bicarbonate of soda and
it will keep odours away.

A really stubborn odour in the fridge can be chased away by
filling an empty coffee tin (leave any residual granules in it) with
charcoal. Leave this in the fridge for a few days, and change the
charcoal every other day until the odour has disappeared.

FRUIT STAINS (on tablecloths)
Dampen camphor and rub over the stain. Wash and that stain
will have disappeared.

Or make a little bag of the stained part and fill it with cream of
tartar. Tie around and boil in soapsuds for a few minutes. Then
rinse as usual.

FRYPAN (cleaning)
Remove dark grease marks from your pan with steel wool dipped
in methylated spirits. Polish with bicarbonate of soda on a damp
cloth for an extra shine.

FURNITURE CLEANER (home-made)
Mix equal parts of vinegar, kerosene, methylated spirits and
turpentine in a glass jar with an airtight lid. Tighten lid and
shake well.

Apply to furniture with a soft dry cloth. Use on any polished
surface for cleaning as it will not damage the basic polish.

FURNITURE POLISH (home-made)

For a wood polish suitable for all woods:

Mix together 1 cup of raw linseed oil, 1 cup of turpentine, 1/2 a
cup of methylated spirits and 1/2 a cup of vinegar. Apply a
little at a time, with a slightly dampened cloth. Buff to shine with
a soft, dry cloth.

G

gilt frames

*restore their lustre
with lemons and baking
powder*

G

GARBAGE BINS

When you put the garbage out do you have to hold your nose?
If so, here's a neat trick - fix a block of deodoriser under the lid
and it will smell a lot better.

GARDEN (compost bins)

Materials NOT SUITABLE for your compost bin:

Meat (encourages rats), **weeds** (the seeds will make their way back
into the garden), **branches**, **twigs**, **detergents**, **diseased plants**
(disease might get back to the garden), **paper**, **dog** and **cat
droppings** and **wood shavings**.

Materials that ARE SUITABLE for the compost bin:

Lawn clippings, egg shells, vegetable and fruit scraps, tea leaves
and **coffee grounds** (these can go straight into the garden),
**chicken bones, seaweed, animal and bird manure, cut flowers,
hair from brushes, dead insects, snails and slugs,
dust ashes from wood fire** (not from coal or paper fire), and
green leaves.

GARDEN PESTS

By planting garlic and sage in your garden it will become less
appealing to destructive insects.

Thyme and mint planted with broccoli or cabbage will keep
cabbage worms away. Geraniums in the garden discourage
Japanese beetles.

GARLIC BREATH
To get rid of the smell of garlic after eating, chew fresh parsley or a piece of celery. Chewing on a coffee bean will also get rid of the strong smell and taste.

To lessen the effect of garlic on your breath, when cooking first remove the centre of the garlic clove before crushing. Cut the clove in half lengthways and ease out the yellow or pale green centre.

GILT FRAMES (cleaning)
Rub over with a piece of lemon. Then add 1 teaspoon of baking powder to half a litre of warm water and sponge frame with it. Rub up with a soft, dry, clean cloth.

GINGER
To keep it fresh, first peel and then wrap in foil and store in the freezer. Grate as needed - it does keep its flavour.

GLASSWARE (cleaning)
For glass ornaments, soak in a container with warm water and a teaspoon of ammonia for an hour. Rinse and leave to dry.

Glasses should be washed with warm water to which a pinch of baking soda has been added. Rinse in cold water with a little vinegar.

Discoloured glass baking dishes will lose any baked on stains when soaked in a solution of borax and water.

GLASSWARE (scratched)
To remove scratches from glasses rub surface with toothpaste and leave to dry. Then wipe away with a clean dry cloth.

Light scratches should be rubbed gently with a dry clean cloth with a few drops of methylated spirits on it until they disappear.

GLUE ON CLOTHES
Sponge with acetone until dissolved then wash. (Avoid fumes and remember acetone is flammable.)

Eucalyptus oil also works wonders.

GOLD (cleaning)
To clean, wash item in soapy water with a few drops of ammonia added. If very dirty, dip item for 5-10 minutes in neat household ammonia, and rinse well.

GRASS STAINS
Sponge white material with a mix of ammonia and warm water. If you don't have ammonia use methylated spirits and water. For fresh stains, rub with methylated spirits or glycerine and leave for an hour. Wash as usual. For old stains saturate with glycerine and soak for an hour. Wash out thoroughly.

GRATER (blunt)
Sharpen a kitchen grater with coarse sandpaper. Rinse and dry well.

GREASE STAIN ON CARPET
Eucalyptus oil dabbed into the stain will help shift it.

GREASY HAIR
Get rid of greasy hair by adding a teaspoon of starch powder to your shampoo, and wash as usual.

GREENFLY
Make a chemical-free spray to get rid of greenfly by dissolving 50g of pure soap oil with a litre of water. Spray the whole plant, especially the undersides of the leaves, at least twice a week with this solution.

GROUTING
To clean tile grouting use an old toothbrush dipped in a solution of bleach and water. If the grouting is very dirty and has become black, clean with a paste of bicarbonate of soda and water applied with a damp cloth.

H

hands

*rub with salad oil before
washing with soapy water
for a gentle cleansing*

H

HAIR BRUSHES
Clean your hair brush regularly by washing in warm soapy water with a few drops of ammonia added. Or shampoo and water will work just as well.

HAIR CONDITIONER
There are a variety of great ways to condition your hair cheaply and using natural ingredients. Apply yoghurt to wet hair after shampooing, leave for a few minutes, and then rinse.

HAIR-DYE STAIN ON BATH OR SINK
Make a paste of peroxide and cream of tartar, cover the stain with paste and leave to dry. When dry wash off.

HAIR LIGHTENERS
Want to lighten your hair naturally, or you've dyed it at home and the colour is too dark ? Use sea water to sort the problem out.

The salt in sea water will act as a gentle bleach, and will reduce the colour gradually. Rinse hair with salt water and leave for as long as you like. Then rinse it out thoroughly and ensure you use a conditioner afterwards, before a final rinse. If you don't get to the beach as often as you want to, fill some plastic water bottles with sea water and take it home for use !

Lemon juice also works as a lightener. Apply to wet hair and for added effect, allow to dry in the sun. This is also a sure way to end up with very dry hair so use a conditioner when washing normally.

HAIR RIBBONS
Children's hair ribbons usually unravel at the cut ends - paint these with clear nail varnish.

HAIR SHINE
There are some great home-made rinses for hair that really do make it shine.

For blonde hair lemon juice (2/3 tablespoons) or a cup of camomile tea added to your final rinse will work.

For red, brunette and black hair, rinse in beer for added brilliance.

Brunettes can also use coffee. Make a cup of espresso, let it cool and then pour it on to your hair. Leave for 5 minutes and then rinse out.

For all hair types, malt or wine vinegar added to your last rinse will remove any last traces of soap, make hair easy to comb and add shine.

HAIR SPRAY (home-made)
Hair spray often contains highly toxic, plastic resins which are harmful to skin, eyes and lungs. Use a non-toxic gel, if you are out of hair spray, or simply make your own using natural, every-day household items. Try either of these two solutions:

Add 2 chopped lemons to a pan with 500ml of water and simmer until lemons are soft. Cool and strain. Put into a pump action spray bottle and keep in the fridge. If you prefer to keep it at room temperature, add a drop of vodka which will work as a preservative. If the mixture becomes too sticky, simply add more water.

Mix a teacup of boiling water with either 1 teaspoon of gelatine or 2 teaspoons of sugar. When cool, pour liquid into a spray gun and spray lightly over hair.

This solution is also great as a setting lotion and can be used over wet or dry hair.

HANDBAG (cleaning)
To keep a leather handbag in tip top condition, rub Vaseline into the bag using a soft nail brush. Buff with a clean dry cloth.

HANDS (cleaning)
The simplest and gentlest way to clean hands is to rub them thoroughly with either Vaseline or salad oil BEFORE washing them in warm soapy water.

Clean garden soiled hands with white sugar and olive oil, rubbed together in your palms. Or wash them with a dab of toothpaste - stains disappear.

Paint is best removed from hands with a soft cloth dipped in kerosene. Then wash hands in warm water with soap.

Nicotine stained hands can be cleaned by rubbing with nail polish remover. For a natural choice, try rubbing with half a lemon. This will help improve the look of cuticles and nail tips too.

HANDS PERSPIRATION
To stop hand perspiring, wash with soap and water, dry and then rub all over with an alum stone.

HARD WATER DEPOSITS
Remove any such hard water deposits from vases, jugs, bottles etc., by filling with malt vinegar. Leave for a few hours, empty, and then rub affected areas with a fine scouring pad.

HEADACHES
Add half a teaspoon of bicarbonate of soda to the juice of a lemon. Mix and drink whilst still fizzing.

HEALTH AND HAPPINESS
Think well of others and always be just and fair in your opinions and actions.

HEAT MARKS
Rub wood that has heat marks with a paste made of cigarette ash and olive oil. Use your bare fingertips and rub well until the marks disappear. Finish with a soft cloth.

HERBAL BATH MIX
Treat yourself to a bath that will relax you and give you a quick pick-me-up.

Soak a few sprigs of fresh mint in a cup of boiling water for 5 minutes. Meanwhile, put some lavender leaves, rosemary leaves and some pieces of orange and lemon rind into a cotton handkerchief and tie securely.

Run the bath with warm water and place the filled handkerchief in it for 10 minutes. Then remove the mint leaves from the cup and add the minted water. Adjust the water temperature to suit you. Climb in and relax!

HERBS
Did you know parsley freezes well. Wash, shake, pat dry, chop and freeze. Chives and basil will do the same.

HICCOUGHS
Moisten a teaspoon of sugar with pure vinegar and swallow.

Place an icecube or piece of very cold cloth against your ear lobe and hold for a few seconds. Repeat at intervals until hiccoughs are gone.

To stop a baby hiccoughing, dip a moistened teat from a feeding bottle into sugar and give to the baby to suck.

I

iron

*remove starch and
stickiness with half a
lemon dipped in salt*

I

ICE-CREAM
Before popping an opened carton of ice-cream back into the freezer, press plastic wrap onto the surface of the ice-cream to prevent crystals forming.

ICE CUBES
Stop your ice cube trays from sticking to the inside of your freezer by wiping them on the outside only with glycerine. Always wipe the sides dry before applying the glycerine with cloth.

If you want to stop your ice cubes from sticking to each other, remove them from the ice cube tray - spray them with soda water and store in poly bags in the freezer.

ICING
If you use all the icing sugar and the paste is still too runny, use powdered milk instead.

ICING (for cakes)
To ice a cake quickly, grate a bar of chocolate and cover your cake with it when you have taken it from the oven.

Another tip when you're in a hurry - place an open-work paper doily on top of your cake and sprinkle well with icing sugar. Remove doily carefully.

ICING SUGAR SUBSTITUTE
Run out of icing sugar ? Make some more by crushing granulated or caster sugar in an electric blender.

INDIGESTION

For relief from indigestion, add a quarter of a teaspoon of bicarbonate of soda to half a glass of hot water and drink.

To avoid indigestion caused by spicy meals, add a little ground ginger to the ingredients.

INDOOR PLANT CARE

A drop of olive oil applied with a cloth to leaves once a week for your indoor plants will keep them healthy. They'll grow faster and the leaves will be shiny and glossy too.

To help new, young plants grow quickly, tie a plastic bag over the pot and leave for a few days at a time.

INDOOR PLANT REVIVAL

Dissolve an aspirin in water and pour on your indoor plant for a perk up!

INK (on leather)

Rub bicarbonate of soda into ink marks and leave for a short time. Dust off and repeat as necessary until the mark has faded.

INK (storing)

By adding either cloves or a few drops of benzine to a bottle of ink, the liquid will stay in good condition for longer.

INK STAINS

Whites only - sprinkle with salt and rub with cut lemon. Leave for one hour, rinse and wash.

With coloured fabric soak in warm milk and then wash in cold water.

This hint also works well for ink-stained clothes; dampen the cloth in warm water and rub a crushed aspirin into the stain. Leave overnight and then wash as usual.

Ink stains should be removed from polished timber floors by washing immediately with water and then dabbing with lemon juice. Dip cotton wool in a weak solution of oxalic acid and place on stain for two minutes. Then wipe off with a damp cloth.

Ink stains on a carpet should be removed by first dabbing with methylated spirits and then sponging with a solution made of a teaspoon of white vinegar, and a teaspoon of detergent mixed in a litre of warm water. Blot the stain and dry with a hair drier.

OR mix a paste of lemon juice with cream of tartar and work into the pile. Leave for a minute and then sponge and blot dry with tissue paper.

INSECT REPELLENT (personal)
Try the following for effective and natural insecticides:

* Vinegar rubbed into your skin. The smell soon disappears, but the taste will linger and insects don't like it.

* Citronella plant. Although some people find the smell too strong and offensive, it certainly is no worse than any insect repellent available from your chemist or supermarket ! It works really well. Crush leaves and rub into skin.

* Tea tree oil and lavender oil work just as well rubbed into the skin.

INSOMNIA
Trouble sleeping ? Try a hot cup of milk mixed with a pinch of nutmeg or cinnamon before going to bed at night.

IRON (cleaning)
To remove starch, or any stickiness on the iron caused by scorching, rub the base with half a lemon dipped in fine kitchen salt.

Burnt man-made fibres can be removed by heating the iron to very hot and scraping off with a wooden spatula. When the iron has cooled, finish with a fine steel wool pad (but do not use this method on a non-stick iron.)

To prevent furring of a steam iron - use only distilled water, or water which has been boiled for 1/2 hour and left to cool (the chalk will settle at the bottom.)

To remove fur from your steam iron, half-fill with vinegar. Heat the iron and press the steam release button until all the vinegar has evaporated. Then fill the iron with distilled or boiled water and repeat the process until the iron is dry. The iron is now clean and ready to use.

IRONING
Clothes are easier to iron if slightly damp

Keep a spray gun full of distilled or boiled water handy and spray both the ironing board and the clothes as you iron.

To give laundry a fresh scent add a few drops of rose water, lemon juice or lavender to the water in the spray gun.

Ironing can be made easier and quicker if a strip of aluminium foil is placed underneath the padded cover.

The strip should be the full length of the board and will heat the clothes from below.

For the perfect pair of ironed jeans turn them inside out and iron. You won't get that extra seam down the side of your leg. Great for any pants not just jeans.

ITCHY WOOLLENS
If a new piece of woollen clothing is itchy to wear, pop it into a plastic bag and leave in the freezer overnight. It will be much softer in the morning, but let it warm up before you put it on !

J

jet lag

immediately adjust your
eating and sleeping patterns
to local time

J

JADE (cleaning)

Wash in warm soapy water, and use an old toothbrush to clean. Dry with a soft cloth. If greasy, rub clean with a little methylated spirits.

JAM (burning)

To stop jam from burning, no matter how fast it is boiled, rub the pan with olive oil before cooking.

JAM (mouldy)

Stop jam from going mouldy by adding a dessertspoon of vinegar to the mixture as it boils.

JAM (runny)

Jam is usually runny because it has not been boiled long enough, or has too much or too little sugar. Add either lemon juice, citric acid or tartaric acid to assist in gelling.

JAM STAINS

Soak in borax and warm water (30g borax to 1 litre water) and then wash.

JARS (cleaning)

To clean smelly jars, fill with warm water and stir in a tablespoon of vinegar and a tablespoon of tea leaves. Leave for a few hours then shake out and rinse. Once dry, they are ready for storage or use. To sterilise, after rinsing, place them in a cold oven (Gas Mark 1, 140°C, or 275°F) for 10 minutes.

JET LAG

There seems to be no known cure for this - but many experienced travellers cope with long distance air travel and the jet lag effects by doing the following:

*   Try (hard but worth the effort) to sleep on the aeroplane at the times suggested by the airline. They set the schedule on board to help you when travelling through different time zones.

*   When reaching your destination, try to adapt to the time zone immediately. Resist the temptation to go straight to bed and adjust your sleeping and eating patterns to local time.

K

kettle

*a clean oyster shell in
your kettle will prevent
furring*

K

KEROSENE FUMES
Get rid of kerosene fumes when using a kerosene heater, by adding a few drops of vanilla essence to the tank as you fill it with fuel.

KETTLE (cleaning)
To prevent a kettle from furring keep a marble or a clean oyster shell inside it.

To remove furring and give the kettle a good clean, half fill with water and add 3 tablespoons of vinegar. Bring to the boil and then rinse thoroughly.

OR Fill kettle with water and add two teaspoons of borax. Bring to the boil, and rinse thoroughly.

KITTY LITTER TRAY
Stop kitty's litter tray from smelling by sprinkling tray with bicarbonate of soda, before putting new litter in tray.

KNEELING CUSHION
Avoid kneeling on hard surfaces where possible, but for those times you need to kneel, protect knees with a cushion. An old hot water bottle, stuffed with old tights or socks makes an ideal cushion. It will protect your knees, it's not slippy and will not damage the surface it is placed on.

KNITTING
Use needles one size bigger when casting off - this will prevent the cast off row from being too tight.

Tooth picks are a perfect way of pinning together pieces of large knitting before sewing up.

KNITTING (dropped stitches)
Use pipe cleaners or small safety pins for holding dropped stitches or stitches that need to be picked up later. The stitches will not slip off or get in the way of your knitting.

KNIVES (sharpening)
Rub small knives against the striking side of a matchbox to sharpen - this works amazingly well. For large knives rub blade vigorously against a stone or clay flower pot.

L

leather shoes

*rub them all over with
a paraffin rag to
remove old polish*

L

LACE (care of)
If white lace is old, wash by hand in warm, soapy water. If very delicate, place in a pillowcase before washing in the same way.

Wash old and valuable lace by shaking in a glass jar half full with soapy lather.

To keep lace fresh store in a warm dry place. Black lace can mould if not aired regularly.

If not used very often, restore white lace by laying it flat on a towel and sprinkle with either talcum powder, bicarbonate of soda, or powdered starch. Rub into the fabric gently with your fingers and leave for 2 hours. Then shake well or brush gently with a soft clothes brush to remove all traces of powder.

To clean black lace, fold garment into a square and place in a container. Cover with beer and soak for 20 minutes. Rinse in lukewarm water before drying. If black lace has a rusty appearance, rinse in a mild solution of ammonia.

LAUNDRY CARE
Wash clothes inside out and hang on the line inside out. They will retain their colour much longer.

LEATHER (care of)
Light coloured leather should be cleaned with petroleum jelly.

To help keep leather supple on chairs and settees and to prevent cracking wipe over with milk. Then dry and polish with a soft cloth.

Stains on leather may be removed with a solution of warm water and vinegar. To finish, polish well with a cloth dipped in linseed oil.

Old leather can be given extra shine if rubbed with a beaten egg white.

LEATHER SHOES
Spruce-up old leather shoes by rubbing them all over with a paraffin rag to remove all old polish. Allow to dry then re-polish in the usual way.

LEMONS
If you submerge a lemon under hot water for 15 minutes before squeezing you'll get a lot more juice out of it.

LETTUCE
You can keep it fresh for up to two weeks and possibly longer if you break off the outside leaves and wrap the lettuce in newspaper. Pop into a plastic bag and place in the fridge.

LETTUCE LEAF SOUP
Don't throw away the outer leaves of your lettuce - save them for soup ! Chop leaves finely and fry in a small amount of butter until soft. Add 1 1/2 cups of milk and 2-3 cups of chicken stock and simmer for 10 minutes. Season to taste.

LIMP LETTUCE
Revive limp lettuce by adding a few teaspoons of sugar to the water when soaking and cleaning. Lettuce will crisp up. Adding the juice of a lemon will also work.

Lettuce should be stored dry in a cold, dark place until needed. Wrapping in paper or foil before refrigeration will help lettuce stay fresh longer.

LINEN (care of)

To minimise discolouration of linen not in constant use - store by wrapping in blue coloured, acid free tissue paper.

Rust stains and discolouration can be treated by first dampening, and then rubbing linen with tartaric acid. Leave in the sun to dry and repeat whole process until stains disappear.

OR wash at a very hot temperature in water to which a tablespoon of cream of tartar has been added.

New linenclothes can be stiff - to reduce stiffness soak in warm water with a few soda crystals and some salt in it.

Linen clothes should be ironed on the wrong side with a hot iron whilst very damp. It is almost impossible to iron out a crease in dry linen.

LINO (cleaning)

To get rid of marks on lino dip steel wool in mineral turpentine and rub well. Then wash in warm soapy water.

LIPS (cracked)

For lips that are already cracked and sore, smear egg white on them and they will soon heal.

LIPSTICK REPAIR

To repair a broken lipstick use a cigarette lighter or match to melt the bottom of the broken piece and stick it to the other piece. Then seal and place in the fridge to cool.

LIPSTICK STAINS

Dab area with eucalyptus oil and then wash as normal.

LOOSE CHAIR COVERS

Cardboard tubes pushed firmly down between the back and seat of loose chair covers will keep the covers tidy and well stretched.

M

moths

thyme, rosemary, lavender
and mint will keep them
away from your clothes

M

MAHOGANY (cleaning)
The best cleaners for mahogany are hot tea or hot beer. Rub
surfaces with a cloth dipped in the liquid. Then polish with a
soft dry cloth.

MAKEUP (application)
When applying foundation to your face, dot it on and then take
some cotton wool dipped in water (or rosewater) and gently
spread evenly over your face. This will obtain a uniform
natural look.

For a natural makeup look, only emphasise the mouth or the
eyes, not both. Older women emphasise the mouth.

Powder your lips before applying lipstick, it will stay on longer
and look neater. Dark lips make you look older, while light
colours make you look younger.

MAKEUP REMOVER
If you have run out of makeup remover grab a raw potato from
the fridge, peel it, slice it and rub gently over your face to remove
makeup. It works!

MAKEUP STAINS
Soak in 1 teaspoon of ammonia to 1 litre of warm water. Then
wash.

MARBLE (care of)
Dull marble can be treated with turpentine. First wash the
marble with warm soapy water and dry. Then rub with
turpentine on a soft cloth and leave for 5 minutes. Finish by
polishing with a clean, soft cloth.

Most stains on marble (except grease and oil) will respond to a treatment of hydrogen peroxide and ammonia.

Sprinkle stain first with hydrogen peroxide and then add a few drops of ammonia. This will cause slight bubbling. Once bubbling has stopped rinse a few times with cold water.

Another good way to clean polished marble is with soap flakes. Soak a cloth in warm water to which soap flakes have been added. Wring out well and then wash surface. Dry with a soft, dry cloth to finish.

Grease and oil stains on marble can be treated with a piece of blotting paper dampened with acetone or nail polish remover. Cover paper with cling film to prevent paper from drying out too quickly and leave for 45 minutes. If the stain is old you may have to repeat the process a few times.

MARKS ON WALLS
If children have left their fingerprints and grubby spots on the wall, try cleaning off with an eraser. Rub gently over the marks - it usually removes most of them.

MASCARA
If your mascara is starting to run out or dry out add a drop of warm water to the container, it will go a little further.

Alternatively, immerse container in a jar or glass of hot water before using to help soften before applying to lashes.

A gentle way to remove mascara from lashes is with a drop of baby oil. Rub the oil between your thumb and forefinger and place at the base of your lashes. Now gently slide down to the tips of your lashes removing the mascara. Tissue off.

MASH POTATO
If you want really fluffy, light mash potato add hot milk to the mashed potato instead of cold. And don't forget the butter and salt - enjoy.

MASSAGE OIL (home-made)
Need an inexpensive oil to massage into those stiff aching muscles? This old fashioned treatment is perfect. You need 1 cup of vinegar, 1 cup of turpentine, 1 beaten egg, a cake of grated camphor, 1 teaspoon eucalyptus, 2 tablespoons olive oil. Place all ingredients into a bottle with a lid and shake well. Leave to stand for a few hours before use. This mixture will improve with age and will keep for years !

MATCHES (damp)
If matches have become damp, and so will not light, dip them in nail varnish and strike (you can do this whilst the varnish is still wet). OR rub them against the bristles of a brush for a few minutes.

MATTRESS
Keep your mattress in tip top condition by making a cover from old sheets. Use elastic at the four corners to hold tightly on to the bed. Fit onto the mattress and lay bed with sheets as normal, on top of it.

Wear a mattress evenly by turning regularly.

MICROWAVE TIPS
Strong smells in the microwave can be removed by boiling water and lemon juice (equal parts) in a teacup for two minutes.

Angel, meringue or sponge cakes are not successful in the microwave. Small biscuits don't work either - they get dry and hard.

When cooking pastry - place a white paper towel over the food and it will be crisper.

Your microwave is great for enhancing the flavour of old spices that have been sitting in the cupboard. Simply put them in the microwave for 30-40 seconds on HIGH before using them.

Another handy trick for peeling garlic, is to place the clove in the microwave for 30 seconds on HIGH. Allow to cool, and the skin will peel off easily.

Be aware of the type of dishes you use in the microwave.
Glass is fine as long as it is strong and does not contain any lead.
Pottery can be used - but avoid anything with a metallic glaze.

Also make sure that any plastic cling wrap you use in the microwave is labelled 'microwave safe' - as other types may give off toxins from the plastic whilst cooking.

This tip is great for giving your microwave a good clean and removing grease and other food spills. Measure a cupful of water into a bowl. Place in the microwave for five minutes on HIGH. The water will boil and the steam will loosen the grease and food stains, which may then be wiped off easily with a sponge.

MILDEW (on clothes)
If clothes have been attacked by mildew, treat as follows:

* Coloured fabrics should be dipped in kerosene, rolled up and left overnight. Then wash in warm, soapy water to which half a cup of ammonia has been added.

* White and light coloured fabrics should be treated by soaking for 10 -15 minutes in a solution of bleach and water, made up at a strength of 1 to 4. Then wash in warm, soapy water.

* Delicate fabrics may be treated by rubbing mildew spots with lemon juice and salt. Keep spots moist in strong sunlight until the spots fade.

* To prevent mildew attack, do not crowd clothing in hanging space.

* During damp, humid weather place a jar of cloves or salt, or camphor blocks in cupboard to absorb moisture.

* Before storing leather goods and shoes leave them in strong sunlight for an hour, then wrap in brown paper or newspaper.

MILDEW (in house)

Mildew in rooms such as the kitchen, bathroom or laundry should be treated with household bleach. Rub surfaces with bleach on a damp cloth, and use a nailbrush for stubborn parts. Once all the mildew has gone, rinse thoroughly with clean water to get rid of the bleach, then wash with ammonia.

Do not paint over mildew on walls as this will not kill it. First wash surface with household bleach.

Prevent mildew in cupboards by washing the inside with a strong solution of bicarbonate of soda and warm water (1 teacup of bicarbonate of soda to 1 litre of warm water). Keep cupboards dry and well ventilated to allow air to circulate.

MILDEW (on leather)

Treat mildewed leather outside. First brush any mildew spots with a clothes brush (do not use the same brush again on clean clothes without first soaking in bleach for 10 minutes and leaving to dry in the sun).

Then wipe the leather surfaces with a cloth dampened with methylated spirits and water in equal parts. Clean with polish and sun-dry for an hour.

MILK CARTONS FOR RECYCLING

Cut cardboard milk cartons in half and use the bottoms for seedlings and cuttings to grow in.

OR tape the top up, place on its side and cut an opening to fill with the seedlings.

For the plastic ones - chop the top off ensuring you retain the handle part and you've got a ready made digging spade with handle for the beach.

MILK SUBSTITUTE

If you've run out of milk for tea or coffee, an emergency trick is to use an egg beaten up to a froth.

MIRRORS (cleaning)

Rub clean with solution of equal quantities of water and methylated spirits.

OR water and vinegar OR salted water. Dry with a crumpled piece of newspaper.

Prevent the bathroom mirror from steaming up by rubbing it with glycerine applied with a soft, dry cloth.

MOHAIR

Use shampoo to wash your mohair garment and it will be soft and fluffy when next worn.

MOSQUITOES

* To stop mosquitoes coming into the house when doors and windows are open, dip cotton wool balls into lavender oil and hang them in mesh bags (from onions, oranges etc.) at the opening.

* Cotton wool balls may also be sprayed with insecticide and hung in this way. This is also effective, but not as pleasant smelling as lavender.

* At night, prevent mosquitoes in the bedroom by adding a few drops of spirit of camphor to a small container and placing on your bedside table.

* When eating outdoors, candles placed on the table will discourage mosquitoes.

MOSQUITO BITE DETERRENTS

Buy a Citronella plant and plant near your outdoor eating area. When the mossies are out and biting break off a leaf and scrunch it up in your hand, rub over your arms, legs and ankles and they won't come near you. Oil of lavender and oil of geranium will also repel mosquitoes.

Mosquitoes do not like the scent of lavender. To prevent them from biting, dab lavender oil on your body behind the ears, knees, on your wrists and ankles.

MOSQUITO BITE ITCH

Get rid of the sting and nasty itch from mosquito bites by applying a mixture of vinegar and bicarbonate of soda to the bite.

Lemon or ammonia applied to bites will also soothe the stinging and a slice of onion placed over the spot will calm and lessen itching too.

MOSQUITO NETTING
If you get a tear in your mosquito net repair with clear nail varnish.

MOTHPROOFING
Stop moths from munching on your clothes by hanging aromatic plants such as thyme, rosemary, lavender and mint in your wardrobe.

Fill the feet of clean old tights or stockings or wrap plants in lightweight cotton handkerchiefs and place in your wardrobe and drawers.

By scattering dried orange peel in your drawers you will keep moths away.

Epsom salts or cloves sprinkled in wardrobes and drawers also keep moths at bay, or wipe cupboards and drawers with a strong ammonia solution before storing clothes in them.

If you have the time you can make spice bags which smell beautiful and are very effective. The recipe: boil together for 15 minutes:

2 cups water, 25g chopped root ginger, 1 tablespoon salt, 1 tablespoon whole cloves, 1/2 teaspoon cayenne pepper, the rind of any citrus fruit and 25g peppercorns.

Strain, and allow to cool, then pop into little cotton bags, tie with ribbon and it's ready.

MOUTH ULCERS
Mum always made us dip a finger into a saucer of bicarbonate of soda, and then hold on the mouth ulcer - it works, they're usually gone the next day.

MUSTINESS

Get rid of musty smells in rooms that have not been used for a while by burning a small amount of eau de cologne in a saucer.

For mustiness in old furniture or cupboards, place an apple stuck with cloves inside and leave for a day or two.

OR use an orange instead - it will have the same effect.

For a closet, try placing several drops of vanilla essence in a saucer and leave on the top shelf for a few days.

N

non-chemical pest spray

protect your plants and the
environment with effective
homemade mixtures

N

NAIL BITING
Paint nails with white iodine at morning and at night for two weeks. The unpleasant taste will stop biting, whilst helping nails to grow and strengthen.

NAIL CUTTING
Nails are best cut immediately after a bath or shower when they are soft and less likely to split. Cut nails with nail scissors that are small and made for the job and file with an emery board.

Always cut toe nails straight across to avoid nails growing into skin.

Keep nails clean when doing a dirty job without gloves, by digging into a piece of soap. The soap caught under your nails will prevent dirt collecting there, and can be rinsed out easily afterwards.

NAIL POLISH (drying)
To dry nails quickly try holding your hands in the freezer for two minutes if you can bear it! Or dip your nails in very cold water.

NAIL POLISH (storing)
Store nail polish in the fridge with the lid shut tightly or upside down in a drawer - it definitely lasts longer.

If you have old bottles of gluey nail polish try dipping the bottle in boiling water for a minute or two. The polish will regain its liquid consistency.

NAILS
To make your nails appear longer when varnishing do not cover
the entire nail - leave a space on either side.

NAILS (weak)
Nails can be strengthened by soaking in room temperature
pineapple juice for 15 minutes a time. Keep juice in refrigerator
to reuse, but bring to room temperature before dipping nails. Do
this every evening or morning for 2 weeks to see real
improvement in strength.

OR soak nails 3 times a week in warm olive oil, for 5 minutes at
a time. Reuse oil.

NAPPIES (cleaning)
Nappy rash can be avoided by ensuring that cloth nappies are
first rinsed and then washed in hot water at 60°C or more. This
will destroy most of the relevant bacteria.

Dry nappies in direct sunlight, as this has a powerful sanitising
effect. Keep nappies soft by adding 2 or 3 tablespoons of
vinegar to the final rinse.

NAPPY RASH
Bacteria breed rapidly in nappies and due to the delicate nature
of babies' skin are often the cause of nappy rash.

Avoid this by changing nappies frequently and wash baby's skin
with clean water between changes. Then gently pat dry.

For a gentle but effective lotion for treating nappy rash, mix
equal parts of olive oil and zinc ointment together and store in
an airtight jar.

Apply to baby's skin directly. Do not use any powder. The ointment will heal and soothe the rash and protect skin from wet nappies. This ointment will stain, so protect nappies with tissues or a nappy liner.

NICOTINE STAINS

Remove nicotine stains from hands by rubbing with nail polish remover. OR Rub fingers with a lemon half.

To remove nicotine from fabrics sponge the stain with methylated or white spirits (dilute spirits with two parts water for man-made fabrics).

Nicotine will come off china if the stain is rubbed with a damp cork dipped in salt.

NON-CHEMICAL PEST SPRAYS

Avoid using chemical sprays in the garden by making your own spray from environmentally friendly substances. Try one of these two solutions:

Boil 2/3 very hot peppers with half an onion and a clove of garlic in a medium size pan of water. Leave to soak for 2 days and then strain the water. This mixture may now be used on both outdoor and indoor plants and will deter pests whilst being harmless to the plants and the environment. To store for future use, freeze and thaw as required.

OR Crush 85g of fresh garlic and soak for a day in 2 tablespoons of paraffin oil. Then dissolve 7g of soap oil in 1/2 litre of water and add slowly to the garlic. Mix and then strain into a glass container. When using, dilute this mixture 1 part to 50 parts water and spray on pests such as insects, worms and caterpillars to get rid of them.

NOSE BLEED
Patient should be seated with head bent slightly forward. Pinch
nose between fingers for 5 minutes, applying pressure on the
bleeding nostril. Then apply a cold compress to nose. This
should stop bleeding, but if it persists visit your doctor.

NYLON (discoloured)
Prevent yellowing of nylon or rayon garments by soaking in
warm water to which a dessertspoonful of bicarbonate of soda
has been added. Then wash as usual.

onions

*plunge them briefly in
boiling water - no more
tears when peeling!*

O

OIL PAINTINGS
Give a favourite (but not too valuable) oil painting a lift by gently rubbing the surface with a cut raw potato.

OLD POLISH
Slightly heated vinegar will remove old polish from furniture.

ONIONS
Store onions in the fridge and they won't affect you when you chop.

To peel onions without crying, first plunge them into boiling water.

OR try putting them in the freezer for an hour or two before they are needed. No more tears when slicing them.

Another tip is to peel from the root upwards or try the one that requires you to put a crust of bread between your teeth.

To remove the trace of onions from your hands, rinse in cold water and then rub with a good pinch of salt.

OPALS
Opals should be dry washed in powdered magnesia. Cover and leave overnight in a container. Brush powder away with a soft brush.

ORANGE JUICE ON CARPET
Pure orange juice will not affect your carpet - just mop it up. However, if the juice has preservatives in it, use soda water as it neutralises the preservative.

OVEN (cleaning)

Make a paste with bicarbonate of soda and water. Rub oven generously with paste, applied with a damp cloth. Leave to dry, then rub off with a clean, slightly damp cloth. Use paste for glass oven door also, but finish off by polishing with a soft, dry cloth to leave glass sparkling.

P

parcel

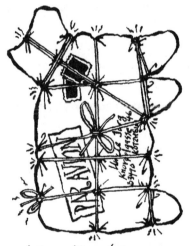

*string dipped in warm
water will shrink and
tighten after wrapping*

P

PACKING A HAT
When travelling, stop hats from being squashed by placing in a plastic bag, blowing up the bag, and sealing securely. The air inside will cushion the hat.

PACKING & PARCELS
When posting fragile objects try popcorn as packaging. It's cheap, environmentally friendly and light.

OR try transporting a small, delicate object in a loaf of bread ! Use the hard, crusty variety and cut in half. Place the object inside one half, taking bread from the loaf as necessary, then place both halves back together. Tape with sticky tape or wrap in a bag to secure.

Wrap a fragile object (such as china) in wet butchers paper. Once dry the paper will harden and form a protective casing.

PAINT BRUSHES (that have dried and hardened)
Soften hard paint brushes in a jar half filled with warm vinegar.

OR leave to soak overnight in a solution of 2 parts water to 1 part ammonia. Wash next day in warm, soapy water, rinse and dry.

Keep paint brushes soft and in good shape by drilling a hole through the handle and threading a length of wire or small twig through it. Suspend the brushes in a jar of white spirits until clean and then in water to rinse. Lastly, empty jar and leave to dry. This will prevent brushes from bending out of shape and allow paint to drain from them.

PAINT DRIPPING

To prevent paint from dripping, place a paper plate with the middle cut out around the top of the paint tin. Drips will collect in the brim and the paper plate can be thrown away when painting is done.

OR Glue a paper plate to the bottom of the paint tin next time you paint - it's a great dribble catcher.

To stop paint from dripping down your hands and arms when painting, wear rubber gloves. Turn the cuffs up and pad with tissue. Drips will flow down the glove and onto the tissue which can be replaced as necessary.

Protect your hair from paint (especially when painting a ceiling) by wearing a shower cap or an old scarf.

A cheap and easy way of protecting clothes from paint spots and spray is to cut holes, for your head and arms, in the bottom of a large rubbish bag and wear it whilst painting!

PAINT MATCHING

Dip an old paddle pop stick into your housepaint and leave to dry. Take the coloured stick with you when shopping for matching curtains, fabrics, furniture or more paint.

PAINT SMELLS

Mix 1 tablespoon of vanilla essence to 1 litre of paint, before applying. This will prevent paint smells in the house.

OR Place 1 or 2 shallow containers full of water to which 2 or 3 tablespoons of ammonia have been added in the room being painted. This will prevent paint smells from spreading to other areas.

To get rid of the paint smell in a freshly painted room, put some slices of cut onion in a bucket of cold water and allow to stand overnight.

PAINT STAINS
Best to remove immediately as these are difficult (if not impossible) stains to remove once the paint has hardened.

Scrape off as much paint as possible with the blunt edge of a knife. Then loosen the stain by rubbing with a little Vaseline. Sponge with turpentine then rinse with cold water and launder as usual.

PAINTING STAIRS
Paint every other step and allow to dry. The unpainted steps can then be used for charging up and down. When dry, paint the remaining steps.

PAINT STORAGE
Before storing half-used tins of paint mark the level of contents on the outside for future reference.

Store upside down as this will prevent a skin forming on the surface of the paint in the tin. (Make sure the lid is on firmly or else you'll have an awful surprise when storing!)

PANS (burnt)
Sprinkle bicarbonate of soda on burnt spot and cover with vinegar. Leave to stand and then scour well.

OR Try bringing to the boil, in the burnt pan, a very strong solution of salt water. Leave to cool for at least 2 hours (for lightly burnt pans) and then rinse. Badly burnt pans may be left for as long as 12 hours, but bring to the boil twice during this time.

PANTYHOSE

How often have you pulled on pantyhose only to ladder them ? To prevent doing this, first dampen your hands and roll each leg down to the foot. Then, roll tights up slowly, one leg at a time.

To adjust to fit properly, re-dampen hands and smooth over legs using the flat palms of your hands and fingers in upward strokes.

Always make sure your nails are smooth with no rough edges to cause a run, before putting on pantyhose.

Keep those expensive, luxury pantyhose for longer, by washing them before wear and spraying with an unperfumed hairspray whilst drying.

For emergencies - keep laddered pantyhose in your bottom drawer and when you need a pair at short notice just chop the laddered leg off and match the good legs.

PARCELS (tying)

Dip string in warm water before tying knot. As string dries it will shrink and make the knot tight.

PASTA

How do you stop the water from boiling over when cooking pasta ? Simply place a wooden spoon across the pan and leave there.

OR A knob of butter in the water will keep the spaghetti from boiling over.

PATENT LEATHER

Best cleaned with a small quantity of warmed olive oil on a soft
cloth. Keep patent leather supple and prevent cracking, by
rubbing with warmed petroleum jelly. Polish with a soft cloth.

PEARLS

To clean pearls and make them look as good as new, place
overnight in a tin of powdered magnesia. Brush away powder in
the morning.

PEARL HANDLES

Never put cutlery with pearl handles in the dish washer and
never use ammonia products on them. Just use warm water and
soap. But never hold them in the water for long as some handles
are glued and the continuing contact with the water will make
them split and crack. Rinse and dry immediately - they will last
for years and years.

PEN MARKS ON LEATHER

Remove pen marks and other hard to remove stains from leather
furniture with nail polish remover. Do this as soon as possible
after the mark is made for best results.

PENCIL SHARPENER (blunt)

To sharpen a pencil sharpener, wrap a small piece of emery
paper around a pencil tip and sharpen pencil as usual.

PERSPIRATION ODOURS

To get rid of any odours left on fabrics, dissolve 2 heaped
tablespoons of bicarbonate of soda in 6 litres of lukewarm water.
Soak garment for an hour, then wash as normal.

PERSPIRATION STAINS

Soak garment in water with plenty of white vinegar or a handful of bicarbonate of soda. Try both and see which one works as they will differ according to your body chemistry.

Sponge old stains with vinegar and fresh stains with ammonia. Rinse and wash in hot water (if possible for the particular fabric).

PEWTER

Dip newspaper in paraffin and rub over the pewter for a good clean. OR using a soft cloth, rub with a paste made of pure white chalk and olive oil. Polish with a clean, dry cloth.

PHOTOGRAPHS (old)

Old photographs can be cleaned with cotton wool dipped in methylated spirits. This will not damage the surface.

PIANO KEYS

Clean ivory piano keys with methylated spirits, lemon juice or eau de Cologne. Do not use water.

PING PONG BALLS (dented)

If ping pong balls are dented (but not cracked), drop them into salted boiling water and stir the balls for few minutes. The dents will disappear.

PLASTIC BABY PANTS

Keep baby's plastic pants soft and supple by adding 1 tablespoon of glycerine to your final rinse.

PLASTIC BOTTLES (disposal of)

Plastic is one of the least environmentally friendly materials and, although it can be recycled, this is not often done because it is cheaper to make new bottles than it is to recycle the old ones. Help keep waste from plastic bottles to a minimum by pouring a small quantity of boiling water into the empty bottle. The bottle will collapse and the plastic will become soft. Crush it in your hands as small as possible before disposal.

PLASTIC BOTTLES (recycling)

Cut large plastic bottles in half, and use the bottoms as containers for storing food in the fridge.

PLATINUM JEWELLERY

Clean platinum by washing in hot soapy water, to which a few drops of ammonia have been added. If very dirty, use pure household ammonia and dip item in it for 5 minutes before rinsing thoroughly. To improve shine, rub with dry baking soda or flour and buff with a soft dry cloth.

PLAYING CARDS

Eventually they tend to stick together. A simple way of extending their life is to lay them out fan-like, sprinkle with talc and shuffle. They'll be slippery, just like a new pack.

PLEATED SKIRT

When packing to travel, draw your pleated skirt through an old stocking (cut the foot out). The skirt will arrive uncreased ready to wear.

POOR POSTURE

Do you suffer from standing badly ? As told many times to children - hold your shoulders back, stick your chest out, and pull your tummy in! Practise doing this whenever you're walking.

An immediate way to improve your posture is to imagine yourself stark naked - it's cheap, simple and you can do it just about anywhere. It's amazing how quickly it will make you pull in those bulges!

PUMPKIN (peeling)
If you put the pumpkin in the microwave for a few minutes the skin will become soft enough to remove easily.

PUTTY
When working with putty, dust your hands now and then with either flour or talcum powder to keep the putty from sticking to your hands.

To keep putty soft for a longer period, keep it in a container of cold water when using, or add a drop of glycerine or linseed oil to the putty and knead in well.

You can make putty with talcum powder and linseed oil, by mixing them together until you get a dough-like consistency.

This is useful in an emergency or as a temporary measure until you get around to doing the job properly.

R

rice

1 cup raw = 3 cups cooked;
a teaspoon of lemon juice will
keep it white + separate grains

R

RAFFLE TICKETS
Do you buy raffle tickets and never know where to keep them?

Staple them into your diary or onto the calendar against the date of the draw, for a simple and efficient system.

RECYCLED PAPER
Quick and easy: chop up old cereal boxes, toss them in the blender with water and blend.

When a thick pasty mess pour out onto wire (A4 size fly screen will do the trick) and press out water by laying a bread board on top and pressing down firmly until all water is drained. Then allow to dry.

When dry, peel off gently and you're ready for scribbling.

RICE
As a rough guide when cooking rice, 1 cup of raw rice will give you 3 cups of cooked rice.

* Add a teaspoon of lemon juice when cooking white rice. This will keep it white and separate the grains.

* Long grain rice does not need washing before cooking - it is already clean and washing it will lose some of the nutritional value.

* Do not stir rice when cooking - it will make the grains stick together.

* If rice is pasty and sticking together after cooking rinse in cold water. The paste will wash away, the grains will separate and you will have perfect rice. Reheat rice with boiling water from the kettle, drain again and serve.

ROCKING CHAIR
Does your rocking chair slide all over the place and leave marks on the floor ?

Glue a thick, strong, velvet ribbon (nylon velvet is fine) to the rockers and this will stop. It will make rocking quieter too.

ROLLER BLIND
Clean roller blinds by removing them from the window and spreading out flat on the floor, on top of newspaper. Sprinkle with white flour or cornmeal and rub the surface thoroughly with a flannel.

RUBBER BATH MAT
Clean your bath mat with vinegar. Pour over mat and leave for 10 minutes or longer if necessary. Brush lightly then rinse with warm water. This will get rid of water deposits and stains.

RUBBER GLOVES
Sometimes rubber gloves are hard to get off, and they stick to your hands. Try running under cold water for a few minutes and then they'll glide off.

Recycle your rubber gloves in the following ways:

Make them into rubber bands by cutting through them, double thickness from top to bottom, including fingers. This will give you colourful rubber bands of different sizes.

The right hand side tends to wear out before the left hand side, so keep the left hand glove for your next pair and re-use, or turn inside out to make a right hand glove.

RUGS
Stop rugs from slipping on polished floorboards by brushing the back edges of the rug with latex adhesive. Leave to dry completely. This will help the rug grip the floor surface.

RUST STAINS
Soak with lemon juice or sour milk and then cover with either salt or bicarbonate of soda. Leave to dry and then wash off in warm, soapy water.

RUST STAINS ON LINEN
Dampen linen and rub with tartaric acid, place in the sun. Repeat until it disappears. Another trick is to treat as before with lemon juice and salt.

snails

lure them away from
your garden with stale
beer

S

SAFETY
After your child is in the car and seat belt fastened make them put their hands on top of their heads. This way you will know where their little fingers are when you shut the door.

SALT AND PEPPER POTS
Clip off the corner of an envelope to make an excellent funnel for use when filling salt and pepper pots.

SALT POT
A few grains of rice added to your salt shaker or cellar will keep salt dry and stop it from clogging. A small curl of blotting paper also works well and does not block the holes, as rice does sometimes.

SALTY SOUP
If your soup is too salty, peel and slice a whole raw potato, and add it to the soup with a pinch of sugar. Boil for several minutes. The potato will absorb some of the salt and can then be removed.

If your soup is too greasy, wrap an ice-cube in a piece of muslin and swish it quickly over the surface of the soup. The grease will congeal and stick to the muslin.

SANDFLY BITES
Equal parts cold tea and methylated spirits will stop the itching.

SANDSHOE ODOUR
Wash with a wool wash and sprinkle inside with bicarbonate of soda. Shake out and make sure you wear cotton socks, this will help absorb the moisture.

SAUCEPANS
To get them sparkling again add two teaspoons of cream of tartar to one quarter litre of water and boil together - this will remove discolouration.

SCALING FISH
Rub with vinegar first and the scales will come off a lot quicker.

SCONES
Milk recently gone sour ? Use it for scone making. Or try substituting yoghurt for milk to give delicious light scones.

SCORCH MARKS
Run under cold water and then soak in warm borax solution. Rinse and wash as normal.

OR try rubbing with white wine vinegar and then rinse with cold water.

SCRATCHES ON FURNITURE
Rub the scratch with a piece of cotton wool soaked in cod liver oil. Leave for several hours and then polish.

Water marks on furniture should be rubbed with a damp cloth dipped in cigarette ash.

White marks on tables caused by hot dishes can be removed by rubbing with spirits of camphor. When dry, polish.

SCUFFED SHOES
Rub eucalyptus oil, using a dampened cloth, into white or light coloured shoes to remove scuff marks, tar and grease.

SEEDLINGS
Cardboard toilet rolls are perfect for growing your seedlings in.

Place upright in an empty shoe box or old ice cream container, fill with soil and plant a seed in each. When the seedlings are ready to be transplanted, you can dig a hole and plant the whole thing. No mess, no fuss.

SEQUINNED FABRIC
Wash in tepid soapy water but make sure the washing powder has dissolved before swishing the garment through. Rinse in cool water and lay on a towel to dry in the shade.

SHAMPOO
If you've run out of shampoo and are desperate, use an egg. The beaten yolk of an egg should be rubbed into the hair and scalp and then rinse off thoroughly with warm water.

SHARPENING SCISSORS
Blunt scissors will cut as good as new if sharpened by cutting through an emery board or sandpaper.

SHEEPSKIN
Sheepskin coats are a classic, so if your coat is second hand you'll need this tip for freshening it up:

Rub the sheepskin lining with a sponge dampened in liquid detergent and it will appear brighter and whiter.

SHELLFISH
Wash all shellfish in very salty water to get rid of sand from them. If you want to get them especially clean and lessen the chance of allergic reactions, poach them in vinegar and water.

SHOE ODOURS
Just put a little dry bicarbonate of soda inside and it acts like a deodorant.

SHOE SHINE
To get an excellent shine on shoes after polishing, use an old pair of pantyhose and they'll sparkle.

SHOWER CURTAINS
Keep mould and mildew at bay by soaking your shower curtain overnight in a bath of bleach and cold water.

A soak in a solution of strong salted water will also work. Rinse and leave to drip dry before re-hanging.

If your shower curtain has become mouldy, sponge with a damp cloth and bicarbonate of soda to remove.

Keep shower curtains soft by adding glycerine to the wash when rinsing them.

SHOWER DOORS (glass)
A solution of equal amounts of kerosene and brown vinegar is excellent for cleaning scum and soap off the glass doors. Make sure the room is well ventilated before you start cleaning as the fumes can be quite strong.

SILK (cleaning)

Dry-cleaning is recommended for all silks, but you can hand wash in mild soapsuds gently. Rinse in cold water and never twist the fabric - simply squeeze gently.

SILK (ironing)

It is best to iron while still damp. Then place on a hanger to continue drying in the seams. If you cannot iron it while still damp, wrap it in a plastic bag and pop in the fridge until you are ready to iron. Don't leave it longer than two hours though. Set the iron on the silk setting and iron inside out.

SILVER

To prevent tarnishing, put a piece of camphor in your silver drawer. To polish silver already tarnished, make a paste of starch and methylated spirits. Wipe on to silver, leave to dry and then polish off.

SILVERFISH

If you have a problem with silverfish treat the area where you have seen them (cupboards, behind furniture etc.) with a mixture of borax and sugar, sprinkled around.

A sprinkling of Epsom salts will also work.

OR try wiping the area with a cloth dampened with turpentine.

SINKS

To get it sparkling again, rub sink when dry, using a dry cloth, with plain flour, cornflour or bicarbonate of soda. At least once a week, pour a saucepan of boiling soda water down the sink to prevent any accumulation of fat which can not only block up your sink, but create a bad smell as well.

But an even better tip is - do not throw anything but water down the sink. This way you will never have a blockage or bad smell and you will be helping the environment by not polluting our beautiful oceans.

SMOKY ROOM
Having a party or dinner and people smoke ? Use candles for lighting and this will keep the room from getting too smoky. A few small containers filled with vinegar and placed discreetly around the room will also work.

SNAILS AND SLUGS
There are gardeners who swear by sawdust as a means of keeping slugs and snails away. If you don't want to use pellets try sawdust.

Sprinkle over soil around your plants. Snails cannot crawl over sawdust it sticks to them and they exit very quickly. Reapply as necessary.

Get rid of snails and slugs in the garden with stale beer, poured into saucers or plastic containers (i.e. margarine tubs) and dug into the garden so that the rim is at ground level. The snails and slugs will be attracted to the beer, dive in and drown.

SOAP
If you're out of liquid soap for handwashing delicates, woollens and silks grate the odd ends of soap and dissolve in water over a low heat. Do not let boil. Cool and it's ready.

SOFT TOYS (cleaning)
Clean the children's favourite soft toy by rubbing cornflour into the fur. Be generous and rub it in well using a soft cloth. Leave for at least an hour before brushing off.

SORE THROAT
Gargle with one teaspoon of salt to one teaspoon of bicarbonate of soda in a cup of warm water.

SOUR CREAM SUBSTITUTE
You need a small carton of natural yoghurt, some single or double fresh cream and lemon juice to make sour cream.

Mix the yoghurt and cream together in equal quantities. Add 4 drops of lemon juice and mix well. The result a great tasting sour cream alternative.

SPECS
Get rid of small scratches on glasses by rubbing toothpaste onto surface with a soft cloth.

SPIDER BITES
Take care when working in the garden during summer and when in bushland.

If you feel a short, sharp pain it is possible that you may have been bitten by a funnel web spider.

Symptoms will include nausea, breathing difficulty, numbness and sweating. In the first instance, apply a pressure bandage over the affected area and **seek medical attention urgently.**

SPLINTERS
To draw out a splinter, cover it with the sticky part of a Band-Aid and leave overnight. When you peel the Band-Aid off the next morning the splinter should come out at the same time, or sufficiently far out for you to get it with tweezers. If the splinter is deeply embedded you might have to do this once more.

SPLINTERS OF GLASS
Pick these up with a pad of damp cotton wool.

SPRAINED ANKLE
A sprained ankle may not seem a serious injury but if not dealt with properly or quickly it can lead to problems that may persist. Remember the emergency treatment as ICE.

I for Ice.
Applied directly to the injury every 2 hours for 15 minutes during the first day or two.

C for compression.
Keep the injury firmly bandaged when not applying ice.

E for elevation.
Keep injured leg elevated as much as possible whilst injury heals.

Even though the ankle recovers fairly quickly it is wise to tape for sporting activities for up to 6 months after injury.

STAINS ON LEATHER
Rub with eucalyptus oil.

STAMPS
To unstick a stamp from its envelope place it in a microwave for two minutes.

STICKY LABELS
Nail polish remover, methylated spirits, or turpentine rubbed over the label will help remove it. Any smudge marks should be rubbed off with the same solution. OR rinse in warm soapy water.

STICKY TAPE

You can't find the beginning of the tape, hold it over the steam of a kettle for a few moments.

STREAKING (clothes)

Prevent dark cottons from streaking in the wash by adding 125ml of white vinegar to the rinse cycle.

This will also help to prolong the life of any stretch fabrics.

STRING STORAGE

Store string in an old tin and punch a nail hole in the top and thread the string through. Now you can keep your string from becoming tangled by simply pulling through the hole and snipping as needed.

SUEDE SHOES

If suede shoes have got spots on them clean with a cloth dipped in glycerine.

SUNBURN

Relieve the itching and soreness of sunburn by soaking in a bathtub of lukewarm water to which a handful of bicarbonate of soda has been added.

SUNSHADE

On a hot, sunny day, drape and peg a large old sheet over the clothes line (Hills Hoist type) to provide a shaded play area for the children.

SWIMMING GOGGLES

How do you stop your swimming goggles from clouding over ? Try rubbing the lenses with baby shampoo - it really works, or else spit on them and rub your saliva into the lenses.

T

threading a needle

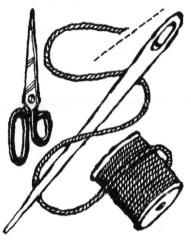

thread cut on an angle
will pass through the eye
of the needle with ease

T

TABLECLOTHS AND TEA TOWELS
Soak in boiling water and cream of tartar (1 tablespoon cream of tartar to 1 litre water) to rid it of all stains.

If a tablecloth is stained during your meal, cover the stain with salt immediately and most of the stain will disappear or at least make laundering much easier.

TABLE SPACE
If you are short on table space use your adjustable ironing board. What I hear you cry! Just cover it with a cloth and place in front of couch - a great table for kids, they'll love it!

TEA CUP STAINS
Rub dry bicarbonate of soda on a damp cup till stain disappears. Salt also works.

TEA STAINS ON LINEN
Use glycerine - it works.

TEA TOWELS
To soften tea towels and make them more absorbent soak in a bucket of water with one packet of Epsom salts. Leave overnight and then wash as normal.

TEETHING BABY
Fill a sterilised teat with water and freeze. Replace it onto a feeding bottle and let baby suck. This will give quick relief.

THICKENING CASSEROLES & STEWS
Try thickening casseroles and stews and savoury pie fillings with instant mashed potato mix. It doesn't go lumpy and tastes great too.

THREADING A NEEDLE
A simple hint that takes a lot of the time and trouble out of threading a needle - when cutting thread, cut it on an angle, diagonally, instead of straight across. The angled edge of the thread slips easily through the eye of the needle.

TICKS
If you discover a tick on your scalp or body do not attempt to pull it off as you might leave the head embedded. Instead cover the tick with Vicks VaporRub and head off to the doctor to get it taken off with tweezers. The VaporRub makes the tick loosen its grip. Bicarbonate of soda is also excellent.

TIGHT LIDS
When a lid is stuck tight and refuses to budge, put a rubber band around it to give a firm grip and try again.

OR tap the sides of the lid a number of times against a solid object (take care only to tap the metal lid) and try again.

OR place the lid between a door and door frame, and holding firm twist lid to open (it may take two of you to do this.)

OR run lid under hot water for a few seconds to expand metal and then twist.

OR grip with sandpaper and twist. If it's still stuck - give up.

TIMBER (cleaning)

Unvarnished, unpainted timber can be cleaned - just wipe over with cool water and detergent, then rinse with a damp cloth. Allow to dry and then coat with linseed oil. Leave for a few hours and then wipe off excess oil.

If the problem is grease build up on timber simply get a bucket of hot water, add a cup of ammonia and wash. Or you could try liquid soap from the hardware store.

TIREDNESS

For a quick pick-me-up press the base of the nose (between the eyes) with the thumb and forefinger and count to ten, slowly.

TOBACCO SMOKE

Whether we like it or not, tobacco smoke pollutes the air and the smell gets into fabrics, carpet, curtains and furniture.

Try getting rid of the smell with one of these methods:

* Leave cider vinegar in a bowl overnight to get rid of the tobacco smell.

* Put 40ml of cloudy ammonia into a bowl and add 500ml of boiling water. Leave overnight in the room (with windows open for ventilation).

TOILET BOWLS

Bet you've never heard this one before - a glass of cola poured down the toilet and left overnight will give you a sparkling loo.

Vinegar is also an excellent toilet cleaner and you'll be helping the environment by not flushing chemicals into the ocean. Leave to soak in bowl for around 10 minutes, then scrub.

TOILET SMELLS
To get rid of unpleasant smells quickly strike a match.

TOMATO JUICE STAIN
Treat an old juice stain with glycerine. Sponge with cold water and then work into the stain and leave for 30 minutes. Then rinse and launder as normal.

TOMATO SAUCE BOTTLE
Don't waste energy shaking and thumping the sauce bottle, only to have sauce finally fall out in huge amounts and splash everywhere ! Push a drinking straw into the bottle through the sauce to the bottom. Remove and the sauce will pour out quickly and evenly.

TOOTHBRUSHES (old)
Keep old toothbrushes for cleaning jobs around the house. They are ideal for cleaning around taps, cleaning jewellery, and for cleaning metal food graters. Use them for any small area that it is difficult to clean.

TOOTH KNOCKOUT
What do you do if you or a member of your family knocks a tooth out ? First find the tooth. If it is clean, put it straight back into the socket from where it came. If it's dirty, wash it in milk before putting it back in. If you have to use water instead, rinse only for a few seconds. Then get to a dentist as quickly as possible. The dentist will likely have to give you a tooth splint and antibiotics, but if you act quickly enough the tooth can be saved.

TOOTHPASTE
If you run out of toothpaste you can make a paste of bicarbonate of soda and lemon juice - brush well.

TOWELS

To make towels fluffy and absorbent soak overnight in the washing machine filled with warm water and half a cup of fabric softener. Next day wash in the same water followed by a cold wash. Dry in a cool place or in the drier.

Another solution to making towels more absorbent is to soak overnight in water and borax (1 litre of water to 1 tablespoon of borax) or warm water and Epsom salts (bucket full of water to half a cup of Epsom salts). Hang out to dry without rinsing.

TRAVEL TIPS

When travelling overseas, there are some very useful and practical tips to follow:

* Always photocopy important travel documents i.e. passport, airline ticket, travel vouchers, travel insurance etc., and keep a note of travellers cheque numbers. Make 2 copies of each. Leave one at home with friends or family and keep one safely with you. An invaluable hint if something is lost or stolen.

* Long before leaving, arrange with your telephone company for a phone card. Most telephone companies offer cards that will work from overseas telephones and the charges will be made to your account with them back home. Again this is a great service to have in an emergency.

* Make sure that friends and relatives know your itinerary and have contact numbers - just in case !

* Keep packing to the minimum. You always end up packing more than you need - and what about room for the shopping?

* If travelling to remote areas or countries where there is risk of personal danger, always make sure you find out where your country's nearest embassy or consulate is - before you depart. In countries where you are warned of danger, it is advisable to call in at the embassy or consulate on arrival and to advise them of your travel plans.

U

uh-oh...

quickly remove stains
with white vinegar

U

ULCERS

Try either of these tips for relief of mouth ulcers:

Dab bicarbonate of soda with a clean finger directly onto the ulcer at any time during the day, but especially last thing before going to bed at night. The ulcer will be soothed and very soon disappear.

Or try this brew - mix 5g of cayenne pepper with 10g of salt, and 10 ml of vinegar. Add to 300 ml of warm water and stir well. Gargle at least twice daily for best results and try not to swallow it !

UMBRELLAS

A rub down with methylated spirits will clean most umbrella surfaces and help them wear better. Follow with a solution of cold tea and ammonia.

For an umbrella that is past its best try this quick renovation tip: dissolve two tablespoons of sugar in half a cup of hot tea and allow to cool. Sponge down your open umbrella with this solution. The sugar will stiffen the fabric and the tea will lift the colour.

If your old umbrella needs help in keeping the rain off, try reproofing by painting the inside with boiled linseed oil.

UNDERARM IRRITATION

If underarm deodorants tend to irritate your skin, try applying hand cream before the deodorant.

URINE STAIN ON CARPET

Soak up as much moisture as possible and then dab on white vinegar. If you catch this quick it will certainly work.

Another tip for dog's urine on carpet is to sprinkle a pack of bicarbonate of soda over stain, leave for 24 hours and then vacuum.

V

vase

*much more stable when
half-filled with
sand*

V

VACUUM FLASK
Clean your vacuum flask inside with this fuss free method. Fill with hot water and add a denture cleaning tablet. Leave overnight, and rinse well before using again.

VARNISH
Stand a tin of varnish in hot water for at least half an hour before using and it will glide on. Apply varnish with the beam of a torch trained on your working area - if your brush has missed any spots you will notice immediately.

VASES (leaky)
Dab clear varnish on that crack or surface of a vase that leaks to make it waterproof again. Make sure the varnish has dried completely before use.

VASES (valuable)
If you're worried about a precious vase being knocked over half fill with sand to make it more stable.

VELVET
To clean dip a cloth in powdered magnesia and rub gently. Or try wiping over with towelling cloth wrung out in warm detergent. Go over again with a clean damp cloth to remove traces of the suds. You can also try carpet cleaner - spray on, allow to dry and then vacuum off.

VERANDAH TILES
To clean them mix 300ml vinegar with the same amount of kerosene. Shake and apply with soft cloth. Also good for paintwork, marble and lino.

VINYL

Cracked vinyl can be repaired by coating with beeswax mixed with equal parts turpentine. Leave for several hours and then polish.

To get rid of black heel marks on vinyl floors put some toothpaste on a damp cloth and rub well - the marks will disappear.

W

weevils

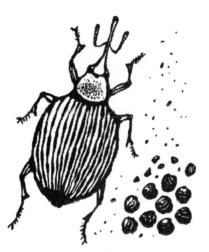

*discourage them with
black pepper*

W

WALLPAPER (application)
Wallpaper sticks better if the wall surface is clean. Use a feather duster or vacuum cleaner to remove all dust. Then wipe the wall down with thick slices of bread - that are 2 days old.

For vinyl wallpaper, vacuum or dust wall and then wipe over with a warm cloth and white vinegar.

WALLPAPER (cleaning)
Make a ball of flour mixed together with cleaning fluid of your choice and rub against marks on your walls to clean. A piece of stale bread will also do the trick.

WALLPAPER (storing)
Do not store rolls of wallpaper standing up, lay them down or you might damage the edges.

Transform ordinary wallpaper into washable wallpaper by giving it a coat of wallpaper sizing, then one of clear shellac.

WARDROBE (freshening)
Keep your wardrobe smelling fresh with spice bags. The following method for making spice bags smells great but is also effective at keeping away moths and silverfish.

Boil together for 15 minutes, 2 cups of water, 25g chopped root ginger, 1 tablespoon of salt, 1/2 teaspoon cayenne pepper, 1 tablespoon of whole cloves, 25g of peppercorns and the rind of any citrus fruit. Strain and then leave the spices to cool. Place into small square of loosely woven fabric, tie at the top with a ribbon and hang in your wardrobe.

WARTS
Castor oil mixed with a little lemon juice, dabbed on several times a day will help get rid of that wart.

WASHING HAIR (children)
To avoid the drama of soap in the eyes and tears at bath time, get your children to wear their swimming goggles in the bath. It's fun and it works !

WASHING MACHINE
You should give your washing machine a clean every three months, try this - fill the machine with water and add one full bottle of vinegar to it. Leave this overnight and in the morning let it run through its full cycle.

WATCHES
If your watch mists up, turn it over and wear the glass next to your skin for a while. The mist will eventually clear.

WATERPROOF WRITING
If you've written on an envelope and you need it to be waterproofed rub it over with a candle.

WATER SAVING IDEAS
Let your lawn grow naturally and cut the grass at least 2.5cm high. This will allow the root system to develop and find water deeper in the soil.

If you must water that lawn then do it only once a week. Water for a short time, allow this to soak in then water again. This will reduce run off.

Also water early morning or evening otherwise it will just evaporate.

Mulching can reduce the water used on your garden. Apply a covering of about 3-4 cms of mulch to moist soil, but leave space around the base of all plants to prevent fungal disease.

An aerating or water efficient shower head can half the water used when showering. The older style shower heads use 20 litres a minute compared to 9 litres with a water efficient one.

A half filled bath uses less water than a long shower. So, take a bath and relax - you're saving water and money.

Plug the sink when rinsing dishes.

WAX (on blackboard)

If your children get carried away and scribble on the blackboard with their wax crayons, wash off with soap and water but follow through by sponging with ammonia to rid the surface of any waxy remains.

WAX STAINS

Wax on fabrics can be removed with ice. Place a block of ice on to the wax. Remove before ice melts. Leave wax for 2 hours and then scrape off.

OR place garment in freezer, leave for half an hour and scrape off wax.

WEATHER FORECASTS

If a ring encircles the moon, expect rain.
If the moon is red, expect wind.
If the moon is bright with a clear sky, good
weather is on the way.
Red sky at night, a beautiful day to follow.
If the sun sets into rising cloud on the
horizon, bad weather is due.

WEDDING ANNIVERSARY
The following is a handy list for that wedding anniversary gift:

ANNIVERSARY	TRADITIONAL	MODERN
1ST	PAPER	CLOCKS
2ND	COTTON	CHINA
3RD	LEATHER, CRYSTAL,	GLASS
4TH	BOOKS, FLOWERS	ELEC. APPL
5TH	WOOD	SILVERWARE
6TH	SUGAR, CANDY	WOOD
7TH	WOOL, PAPER	DESK SET
8TH	BRONZE, POTTERY	LINEN, LACE
9TH	POTTERY, WILLOW	LEATHER
10TH	TIN, ALUMINIUM	DIAMOND JEWELS
11TH	STEEL	FASHION JEWELS
12TH	SILK, LINEN	PEARLS, GEMS
13TH	LACE	TEXTILES, FURS
14TH	IVORY	GOLD JEWELLRY
15TH	CRYSTAL	WATCHES
20TH	CHINA	PLATINUM
25TH	SILVER	SILVER
30TH	PEARLS	DIAMONDS
35TH	CORAL	CORAL
40TH	RUBY	RUBY
45TH	SAPPHIRE	SAPPHIRE

WEEDS
The best tip for this is hard work - keep pulling them out as they appear and eventually you'll beat them.

Kill weeds on footpaths or patios quickly and easily by pouring boiling water from the kettle directly onto them.

WEEVILS
Weevils usually get into packaged foods such as cereal, flour and rice, as eggs. These eggs hatch when the temperature and humidity are right.

If bought in small enough quantities, freezing any of these products, before storing, will usually kill the eggs. Freeze for a few days before you need to use, then store them in sealed containers at room temperature.

There is no health hazard directly associated with weevils, but washing rice, pasta etc. before cooking will get rid of any trace of them.

Try and keep weevils out of your cupboards by hanging black pepper, in small cloth bags, inside them.

WHITE CORRECTION FLUID
For those small chips on white surfaces such as the bath, fridge or woodwork, dab some white correction fluid on the spot and leave to dry.

WHITE PAINTED WOOD
This is just a quick repair - use white shoe polish to hide scratches on white painted wood.

WHITE SAUCE
Stop it going lumpy by adding a tablespoon of cold water to the butter and flour before you add milk and you'll never get lumps.

WHITES (yellowing)
Soak white clothes and linen that has yellowed in borax and cold water for several hours. Then launder in hot water and dry in the sun.

WICKER FURNITURE
A cloth moistened with a little oil and rubbed over your outdoor wicker furniture will protect it from the weather.

WIND
This is an old tale but worth a try if you have a wind problem: Eat burnt toast.

WINDOW BOXES
Instead of watering with water and letting it all run out of the bottom place ice cubes on top of the soil for a slow watering and less mess.

WINDOW FRAMES
When painting window frames, a way to avoid getting paint on the glass is to use a strip of cardboard held close to the frame and laid flat.

Another way is to use strips of newspaper dampened with warm water and laid on the glass around the frame, secure the corners and paint away.

WINDOWS (how best to clean them)
An effective simple recipe for window cleaner is equal parts water and methylated spirits. Shake this or mix well. Damp a newspaper with this and rub on windows or mirrors. Follow this by polishing with a soft cloth.

Bird droppings are always difficult to get off glass, usually the windscreen of your car. Rub with a cloth soaked in vinegar and it will come off in a flash.

Do not use soapsuds or detergents to clean your windows. We've tried it and the windows looked dirtier than before and were covered in streaks.

For sparkle add several drops of ammonia to the water.

The cheapest and most efficient way to clean windows is my grandmother's - wet newspaper.

WINDOW SCREENS (and flyscreens)
To clean window screens, lay them on a flat smooth, cloth covered surface. Scrub gently with soapy water and rinse with a hose and let stand to dry.

WINE
Never store bottled wine upright, always store on its side, as the cork becomes dry and the wine might become tainted.

Cooking wine will store longer if you add a few drops of olive oil to it.

If white wine is required for making a sauce and you don't have any, use one tablespoon of white wine vinegar, with half a tablespoon of sugar and two tablespoons of water and mix well. And that's it!

WINE STAIN
Quickly cover with salt and then soak in cold water for an hour and wash as usual. You can also soak in borax and warm water.

Another trick is to hold the stained portion of the cloth in boiling milk (use a wooden spoon).

WOK
To stop it rusting when not in use, wash and dry it then warm up several drops of oil in it. Now rub this oil all over the wok with a paper towel. Store when cooled down.

WOOD
Wash painted wood with a diluted solution of sugar soap. It'll look like new again.

WOODEN CHOPPING BOARDS
OR BREAD BOARDS
To keep these in good condition wipe with a cloth dampened with oil when your board is clean and dry.

You've just rolled out dough on your board - it's always hard to clean off isn't it? Not if you sprinkle your board with salt and rub the sticky dough away with your hands.

To get rid of smells like that cut onion on your board rub with half a lemon.

WOODEN FRAMES
If you're bored with your natural wooden frame try this. Make a strong pot of tea and when cool use it to stain the frame - it looks great. Cover afterwards with wax or a layer of varnish.

WOODEN FURNITURE (that's old)
A great wax recipe for old wooden furniture is a mixture of linseed oil, methylated spirits and vinegar (equal parts). Shake together and now rub on with a soft cloth. Leave to dry for roughly eight hours and then buff.

WOODEN SALAD BOWLS
When cleaning always only rinse in cold water. Occasionally you can clean with a warm oil and then dry this off with a paper towel.

Another tip, always use wooden salad servers for tossing and serving, as these do not bruise the leaves.

WOODEN TABLES
If your favourite wooden table is unvarnished rub it often with salad oil and polish. This will keep the wood from becoming brittle.

WOODWORM
Inject each hole with turpentine until saturated. Close hole with wax or furniture polish. (Use a hypodermic syringe for injecting the holes.)

WOOLLENS
Shrunken woollens can be re-stretched. Dissolve Epsom salts in boiling water, let cool and pop garments in - leave to soak for half an hour. Squeeze out excess water and shape and leave to dry flat on a towel.

To stop them itching when worn against the skin add five teaspoons of castor oil to the final rinse or several tablespoons of glycerine to the last rinse.

Wash mohair jumpers in hair shampoo.

WRINKLES IN CLOTHES
If you're travelling and you are not able to press your clothes, run a bath with hot water, hang your clothes in the bathroom and close the door. The steam will remove a lot of the creases.

WROUGHT IRON
To keep wrought iron in perfect condition brush with a natural wax and then shine up.

Y

Yorkshire pudding

*add hot milk when
mixing and it will be
light and crisp*

Y

YELLOWED WHITES

Whiteness may be restored to yellowed clothing by adding a teaspoon of turpentine to the water in your wash.

Certain fabrics, such as net curtains, collect dust and dirt and can become discoloured.

To renew yellowed curtains soak the fabric in a bucket of warm water to which you add a cup of cream of tartar. Leave for 24 hours and then tip into your washing machine and wash on a warm soapy cycle and rinse.

After time, especially for sporting whites i.e. cricket, tennis, the fabric may become tired and yellow in colour. To revive, try sponging with cloudy ammonia or cover with a thick paste made with water and starch. Leave to dry then brush off and wash as usual.

Alternatively, try dampening the clothes, and then covering thickly with borax and leave for a few hours. Rinse well and then soak overnight in a nappy treatment. Launder with hot water to finish and for a bright, white look.

YOLKS

When cooking and only using the whites of the egg - store yolks until ready for use by putting them in a glass. Then melt a little butter and whilst it is still warm - but not hot - pour over the egg yolks. Keep in the fridge.

YORKSHIRE PUDDING

To make it light and crisp use hot milk when mixing the flour, egg and milk.

Another trick is to add a few drops of olive oil to the mixture, just before placing in the oven.

zippers

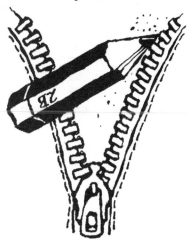

rub them with a lead
pencil and they will open
and close smoothly

Z

ZINC CREAM STAINS

Rub with a prewash cleaner and then soak for one hour, rinse and wash as normal.

ZIPPERS

If they are difficult to close, rub with paraffin wax or try sprinkling with talc. Soap or candlewax also works, as does rubbing a lead pencil up and down the teeth of the zipper.

GLOSSARY

ACETONE (from chemists) A highly flammable solvent. Good for removing paint, oils and nail varnish. Do not use on acetate fabrics.

ALCOHOL (from hardware shops and chemists) Organic chemicals, methylated spirit and surgical spirit are forms of ordinary rubbing alcohol. These solvents are good for removing stains on fabrics. Dilute the alcohol in two parts water for man-made fabrics. First test if dyes are affected by the alcohol.

AMMONIA (from hardware shops) Alkali and grease solvent. Gives off strong fumes, so use in a well-ventilated room and wear rubber gloves. Store in a cool, dark place. Buy cloudy household ammonia as it has a little soap added to it. It's great for removing grass, chocolate and blood stains from fabrics and as an oven cleaner. Do not use ammonia and bleach together - together they release a dangerous gas.

BICARBONATE OF SODA (baking powder from supermarkets) Very useful for cleaning paint, ovens, glass, fridges and china. Removes stains from fabrics. Cleans teeth and jewellery. A definite must-have in the house - buy the biggest pack available. Bicarbonate of soda is also friendly to the environment.

BLEACH (household bleach from hardware stores and supermarkets) Very useful for bleaching white linen and cotton. Do not use on wool or silk. Can lose effectiveness if stored too long.

BORAX (from chemists and supermarkets) It is a compound of mineral salt which is a combination of boracic acid and soda. Is a substitute for chlorine bleach. It loosens dirt and grease and is also good as an antiseptic. Effective cockroach and ant poison. Note it is toxic to plants.

BRAN (from supermarkets and health food stores) The husk of grain sifted from flour, after grinding. Used hot or warm as an absorbent to clean felt and velvet.

CAMPHOR & SPIRITS OF CAMPHOR (from supermarkets) White, translucent, crystalline substance.

CASTOR OIL (from supermarkets, chemists and health food stores) Obtained from the seeds of the castor oil plant. Great for cleaning leather.

CREAM OF TARTAR (from supermarkets) A white powder, extracted from the deposits of wine after fermenting in the production of wine and refined.

COD LIVER OIL (from chemists) Oil extracted from liver of common cod or allied species, extensively used in medicine as a source of vitamins A and D.

EPSOM SALTS (from supermarket, and chemists) A white powder made from magnesium sulphate.

ESSENTIAL OILS (from health food shops, department stores) Are great as perfume for home-made cleaners and as natural insect repellents.

EUCALYPTUS OIL (from supermarkets, chemists and health food stores) An aromatic straw coloured oil. Used in medicine as an inhalant. Brilliant for removing grease on any fabric, even the most delicate.

GLYCERINE (from chemists and health food stores) An odourless, clear liquid which is a good solvent to loosen many kinds of stains on fabric.

HYDROGEN PEROXIDE (from chemists) A clear liquid for cleaning particular surfaces and fabrics. Use 20 volume strength and store in the fridge.

KEROSENE (from hardware store) A flammable fuel. It is mixture of liquid hydrocarbons obtained in the distillation of petroleum, used for lamps, engines, and heaters.

LINSEED OIL (from chemists and hardware shops) Comes from the common flax seeds. Normally used in oil paints, varnishes and polishes. Highly flammable.

METHYLATED SPIRITS (from hardware stores, supermarkets and chemists) A grease solvent that is highly flammable so handle with care. Use in small amounts and only if really necessary try vinegar first. Do not use on French polished surfaces it will dissolve the polish.

NAPPY TREATMENTS (from supermarkets and chemists) The active ingredient is bicarbonate of soda, mixed with detergent and brighteners. A bulking agent is also added.

PARAFFIN (from hardware stores) A flammable fuel used for cleaning and heaters.

POWDERED MAGNESIA (from chemists) A powder derived from magnesium carbonate.

SADDLE SOAP (from saddleries) Used as a leather conditioner, made primarily of glycerine.

SODA WATER (from supermarkets) An effervescent beverage consisting of water charged with carbon dioxide

SULPHUR (from chemist) A non-metallic element, usually sold in powder form.

TARTARIC ACID (from supermarket) A substance made from the juice of grapes, after they have been fermented in wine producing. Then refined.

TURPENTINE (from hardware stores, chemists and supermarkets) Turpentine, is an oil derived from pine trees and mineral turpentine is petroleum-based. Flammable and used as a solvent for wax, varnish, paint etc. Neither is toxic but please don't pour down the drain or sink.

VASELINE (from supermarkets and chemists) A soft greasy substance used on metal as a rust preventative and for conditioning leather. Also used to loosen heavy grease stains on fabric prior to a solvent.

VICKS VAPORUB (from chemists & supermarkets) Contains menthol, camphor, turpentine oil, eucalyptus oil, cedarwood oil, nutmeg oil and thymol.

VINEGAR (from supermarkets) White vinegar is a mild acid and great cleaning agent. It dissolves dirt and softens water. It is an excellent stain remover and effective disinfectant. It is produced by the fermenting of one or more of the following: honey, glucose, malt, spirit, cider, wine, fruit, molasses and alcoholic liquors. Vinegar is environmentally safe.

INDEX

woollens, 158
woollens, itchy, 74
writing,
waterproof, 151
wrought iron, 158

Y
yellowed
whites, 160
yolks, 160
yorkshire
pudding, 161

Z
zinc cream
stains, 164
zippers, 164